In the Beginnings

Foundations for the Millennium Ahead

ALSO BY JAMES L. DOHERTY

Race and Education in Richmond

Faith Is Alive in You

In the Beginnings

Foundations for the Millennium Ahead

James L. Doherty

Brunswick

Cover art by Madeleine Pydych Hopkins

Library of Congress Cataloging-in-Publication Data

Doherty, James L. (James Louis), 1932-
In the beginnings : foundations for the millennium ahead / James L. Doherty. — 1st ed.
p. c.m.
Includes bibliographical references and index.
ISBN 1-55618-178-7 (pbk. : alk. paper)
1. Conduct of life. 2. Values. I. Title.
BJ1581.2.D64 1999
170'.973—dc21 99–28060
CIP

First Edition
Published in the United States of America
by

Brunswick Publishing Corporation
1386 Lawrenceville Plank Road
Lawrenceville, Virginia 23868
1-800-336-7154

A Background Note and Some Thanks

Please consider this book an introductory text. Each of the six essays contains a synthesis of ideas to provoke appreciation and encourage further study of the basic elements critical for the health of the United States.

Thanks go to Earle and Jane Dunford, who have proofread and diligently edited the three books I have written. Charlie and Alice Todd are great pals, who contributed their thoughts after reading each chapter twice. They along with my son Paul suggested the bibliography so that readers would recognize this book as a primer. Tom Howard refined the manuscript. Tom and my sister-in-law, Dianne Doherty, suggested a more compelling "expository" message, which follows. Charlie Finley, Jr., served as a consultant in the design and marketing of the book. Madeleine Pydych Hopkins, a daughter of a lifelong friend, drew the family scene for the cover.

I dedicated my first two books to my wife, Mary Lou. She has played mankind's quintessential role—the nurturing and preservation of the species. Mary Lou blessed me with four children—Louis, Frank, Mary Beth, and Paul—and then raised them to become healthy adults. Three are now married. I dedicate this book to her.

James L. Doherty
Richmond, Virginia
March 1999

PREFACE

I am a sucker for values.

Ronald Reagan's acceptance speech following his nomination for President at the Republican National Convention in July 1980 inspired me. Reagan sought to evoke the best in America in " a community of values embodied in these words: family, work, neighborhood, peace, and freedom." In his 1984 State of the Union address, President Reagan added faith to the community of values.

Four years later I drafted an outline entitled "back to the basics" for a book consisting of an essay on each of these values. I cited President John F. Kennedy, whom I likewise viewed as an inspirational leader. In a text deterred by assassination, Kennedy was to have told an audience in Austin, Texas, "Our duty as a party is not to our party alone, but to the nation and, indeed, to all mankind. Our duty is not merely the preservation of political power but the preservation of peace and freedom."

The chapters ahead are intended to begin to define and flesh out these assets, which I believe essential to the health of the nation. To the extent they are upheld in America, individuals, communities, and country will flourish. The United States today is viewed as the sole superpower. Those abroad have their eyes on Americans—you and me. The whole world will benefit as you, your family, Democrats and Republicans, set standards for the coming millennium by promoting peace, freedom, work, faith, family, and neighborhood.

When reviewer Tom Howard read the essay on peace, he thought the message took the position of a pacifist and conscientious objector. He had just returned from Ireland and wished retribution and justice for the terrorists whose bombing had taken the lives of children. I favor capital punishment and a strong national defense posture—having served a 16-month tour in Korea. The essay on freedom attests to the eternal struggle between liberty and equality. The American promise lies not in equality but in the pledge of allegiance with "liberty and justice for all." President Reagan could have added justice as the seventh element in the creed.

I encourage readers to take a chapter at a time and pause for reflection. Read each chapter when the spirit moves you, or, if you are open to a suggestion, schedule your reading to coincide with special events and holidays. The essay on peace could be read on Memorial Day; that on freedom, on Independence Day; and that on work, over the Labor Day weekend. I suggest the essay on faith for the holiest day in your tradition and those on family and neighborhood at reunions, weddings, and community celebrations.

As you read, I invite you to question, think about, appreciate more, and resolve to support each value.

You could take a cue from my own experience. In 1992 I sent the outline for this book to Charles Walton, a California resident. He responded by calling President Reagan's talk of peace and justice total hypocrisy. He challenged me to follow his example(see page 11) in supporting a peace essay contest among high school and secondary school students. In 1996 our family established an endowment fund to further the causes of education, faith, freedom, peace, and other elements basic to the well-being of the community in the Richmond, Virginia region.

The first grant from the Doherty family fund in 1998 was directed to the Richmond Peace Education Center for the conduct of an essay contest among students. The contest elicited 255 responses from young people and an editorial column by an essay reviewer in the *Virginian-Pilot* newspaper.

I hope that the six essays will stir you to reflect and act on these values.

Table of Contents

On Peace

"Grace be unto you, and peace from God," wrote Paul as he addressed his friends in Corinth and Ephesus. Ave peace.

How does a mortal create peace, the foundation of a great society and personal contentment? Confucius, preceding Paul (and ignoring God), had written:

> The ancients who wished to illustrate the highest virtue throughout the empire first ordered well their own states. Wishing to order well their states, they first regulated their families. Wishing to regulate their families, they first cultivated their own selves. Wishing to cultivate their own selves, they first rectified their hearts. Wishing to rectify their hearts, they first sought to be sincere in their thoughts. Wishing to be sincere in their thoughts, they first extended to the utmost their knowledge. Such extension of knowledge lay in the investigation of things.
>
> Things being investigated, knowledge became complete. Their knowledge being complete, their thoughts were sincere. Their thoughts being sincere, their hearts were then rectified. Their hearts being rectified, their own selves were cultivated. Their own selves being cultivated, their families were regulated. Their families being regulated, their states were rightly governed. Their states being rightly governed, the whole empire was made tranquil and happy.

More than two millennia had elapsed when Pope John XXIII promulgated his encyclical *Pacem in Terris* in 1963. He appealed to all men of good will. Despite the counsel of

Confucius, the states had not been tranquil over the intervening centuries, nor had men of good will necessarily prevailed.

War has blighted the planet in all but 268 of the past 4,000 years. For every year of peace in mankind's history, there have been 14 years of war. In this century, 40 million people have died in international wars while 100 million have been killed by their own government. Near a recent Memorial Day, the toll of the U.S. War dead was recounted.

The graves of the 1,153,541 Americans killed in war stretch across the country and around the world. More have been killed by Americans than by any single foreign foe.

- Civil War — 497,000
- World War II — 406,000
- World War I — 116,000
- Vietnam — 58,000
- Korea — 54,000
- Mexican War — 13,000
- Revolutionary War — 4,000
- Spanish-American War — 2,400
- War of 1812 — 2,000
- Indian wars — 1,000
- Persian Gulf — 141

"The staggering and terrifying thing about war is that, despite the loathsome things said of it on one side, and on the other, despite the noble causes and holy reasons and high ideals brought in to prop it up, one fact stands alone: war has been popular," Joseph Campbell wrote. He concludes a chapter on the mythology of murder, "The ability to wage war and to impose collective human sacrifice has remained the identifying mark of all sovereign power throughout history."

On Human Nature

Pope John's encyclical prompted men and women to convene two years later for a colloquium. Paul Tillich, a theologian, commended the Pope for citing the primacy of the individual both in rights and duties to foster peace, but he thought the Pope had erred in addressing his remarks to "men of good will." Rather "one should appeal to all men knowing that in the best there is an element of bad will and in the worst there is an element of good will. The view of the ambiguity of man's moral nature has direct consequences for the way a peace conference should look at the chance for a future state of peace."

A participant claimed man is both a saint and a killer. In another forum, George Steiner sought to explain

> ... the fabric of history, which is hellish.... If one would endeavor to experience as at all intelligible the recursive onset of evil, of self-destructive barbarity which pulses through both public and private historical-social existence—the live-burial politics of Pol Pot, the battering of the child in countless homes—one does better, I conjecture, to look at Kant's postulate of incarnate evil than, say, to the promissory meliorism of Locke or John Stuart Mill. More specifically, it is the Augustinian reading of original sin, of history as the enactment of some radical (at the roots) deflection from grace, which looks to be far truer to the blatant facts than any other hypothesis.

Violence was present at the outset of recorded history. Cain slew Abel. Hannah Arendt notes in *On Revolution*, "Whatever brotherhood human beings are capable of grows out of fratricide."

Other students of human behavior claim that war is instinctive. In 1973, the Nobel Prize judges chose Konrad Lorenz as the recipient of a prize in physiology and medicine. Lorenz had written a book, *On Aggression*, in which he declared that all species had warring instincts. Man was just one of an infinite number of living organisms that had certain common elements. The tendency to fight, to be aggressive, was one ingredient in the genetic code. (Editorial comment: Lorenz counseled games, such as chess and tennis, as a means of expressing that instinct. Peace devotees tend to stress the importance of cooperation, the focus of this essay, leading to the implication that cooperation is preferable to competition. In the author's judgment, the two forces are equally valid and meritorious. Also, Lorenz made no distinction between the sexes, a matter to be addressed later in this essay.) In 1894, seven Nobel laureates, Lorenz' predecessors, gathered among 77 men from 14 nations to revive the Olympic Games, a peaceful enterprise centered on competition.

Myths endure. From Prometheus to Faust, parables trace the germ of violence, starting with a man who, of free choice, sought and stole power to set loose enormous goods and great evils in the world. Faust stood for an ideology that purports that man can command not only the physical but the social environment as well. Mere men and women can transform by physical action not simply the earth, but the qualities of the creatures who dwell upon it. Westerners hold that the world of history and time is a thing to be manipulated and won.

Steiner looked to Kant for an explanation of violence. Kant claimed that strife of each against all represented nature's method of developing the hidden capacities of life; struggle is the indispensable accompaniment of progress. In *The Story of Philosophy*, Will Durant paraphrased Kant's exposition put forth two centuries earlier:

> If men were entirely social man would stagnate; a certain alloy of individualism and competition is required to make

> the species survive and grow. Without qualities of an unsocial kind...men might have led an Arcadian shepherd life in complete harmony, contentment, and mutual love; but in that case, all their talents would have forever remained hidden in their germ.

Durant continued to quote Kant:

> Thanks be then to nature for this unsociableness, for this envious jealousy and vanity, for this insatiable desire for possession and power... Man wishes concord; but nature knows better what is good for the species; and she wills discord, in order that man may be impelled to a new exertion of his powers, and to the further development of his natural capacities.

(In a subsequent essay, Kant stated it was time that nations should emerge from the wild state of nature and contract to keep the peace.)

George Will, in a nationally syndicated column, numbered Machiavelli among the five most significant figures in western history. Arendt described Machiavelli, who insisted on violence, as "the spiritual father of revolution." In *The Politics of Hysteria*, Edmund Stillman and William Pfaff traced the germ from Prometheus to Faust claiming cases of total war by non-western societies are rare. Other cultures have limited their engagement to clearly defined ends. Clausewitz, the father of the textbook on the conduct of war taught at West Point and Annapolis, countered with barbarities; "to introduce a principle of moderation would be an absurdity. War is an act of violence pushed to its utmost bounds."

Jawaharial Nehru, noted Pfaff and Stillman, observed that the violence of the capitalist society resting on material acquisition is inherent. Erich Fromm confronts the matter in *To Have or To Be.* He contended that so long as people are driven to "having things, through consumer spending; the seeds of war are being sown.... The idea that one can build peace while encouraging the striving for possession and profit is an illusion."

When the demon in man is coupled with a destructive ideology, war follows. Reason vanishes and extravagant cruelty accompanies the pursuit of an unattainable idea—whether Marxist, Catholic, Protestant or Aryan. In medieval eras, crusaders fought against heresy. The 16th and 17th centuries saw wars of religion. Hitler aimed to manipulate life itself through the eradication of Jews. An English member of Parliament in rejoinder said, "I'm all for the bombing of working class areas in German cities. I am Cromwellian. I believe in 'slaying in the name of the Lord'. "

Nation Founded on Revolt

"Life, liberty, and the pursuit of happiness," declared the nation's forefathers as the purpose of the republic, the newly created United States of America. Patrick Henry reversed the first two elements in the creed with a stentorian voice proclaiming that without liberty, life was not worth living. The commitment in this instance was to freedom, an ideology, according to Arendt, that had not held root since Greek and Roman antiquity. So children in American classrooms today read the story of the nation's founding out of revolt and admire the father of the country for his steadfastness at Valley Forge.

When Washington led his men, only the combatants' lives were at risk. The nature of war has changed in the interim. World War I witnessed 30 million casualties. The seeds of total war emerged, and the distinction between soldiers and civilians vanished. The army no longer defended the civilian population. The invention of explosives had led to the practice of violence on a truly Titanic scale.

Hiroshima. Nagasaki. Now the stake became not Christian, Muslim, Hindu, or Jewish but human civilization. The fate of the earth and the species charged with the Old Testament announcement of dominion over it had become the issue.

The Just War?

Pope John XXIII called for peace. But what about tyrants? Tillich observed that Catholics had traditionally distinguished between just and unjust wars. There are circumstances in which the right to exist might lead first to rebellion, then to revolution, then to war. Augustine so argued in the fourth century. In *The City of God*, he wrote,

> It is quite fitting for good men (men of good will) to rejoice in an extended empire. For the iniquity of those (men of bad will) with whom just wars are carried on favors the growth of the kingdom.

For Augustine, men fight to restore peace. He stated,

> War should be waged only as a necessity and waged that through it God may deliver people from that necessity and preserve them in peace. For peace is not to be sought in order to rekindle war, but war is to be waged in order to obtain peace. Therefore even in the course of war you should cherish the spirit of the peacemaker.

Thomas Aquinas and subsequent apologists developed seven criteria to justify war: (1) just cause, (2) right authority, (3) right intention, (4) overall proportionality of the good to be done over the evil, (5) reasonable hope of success, (6) situation of last resort, and (7) the goal to restore peace. In the application of those tests to the 1991 fracas in the Persian Gulf, a *Christian Century* contributor contended that the means should be discriminate and tactically proportionate.

Moral principle holds that noncombatants should be protected from intentional targeting by military force. Iraq's directing of SCUDS at bystanders such as Israel and Saudi Arabia violated that principle. He also noted that the ability to make closely targeted strikes against military installations had produced a "very different kind of war."

The Jewish tradition holds for the right of self-defense. Despite Jewish abhorrence of war and belief in the sanctity of human life, Jews may take a preemptive attack against an aggressor (to erase a nuclear threat from Iraq). War had been religiously commanded for the original conquest of the land of Israel. Martin Buber explained the Jewish view in a 1939 letter to Gandhi,

> We have not proclaimed, as you do and as did Jesus, a doctrine of non-violence. We believe that a man must sometimes use force to save himself or even more his children. But from time immemorial we have proclaimed the teaching of justice and peace; we have taught and we have learned that peace is the aim of the world and that justice is the way to attain it. Thus we cannot desire to use force.... But if there is no other way of preventing the evil from destroying the good, I trust I shall use force and give myself up into God's hands.

Pacifists rightfully laud Gandhi as a paradigm of the force of passive resistance. Skeptics wonder if the Mahatma would have prevailed or even survived if he had encountered tyrants, men empowered by evil consciences.

Peace and War Defined

What is peace about—those years noted for their tranquility? Western languages trace the etymology of the word to a lull, the absence of strife. In the Greek translation, the term, from which Irene and irenic are derived, is defined as a truce.

Pax, which Pope John XXIII hailed, means an agreement, a compact arising from the struggle between conflicting interests.

In other traditions and cultures, peace has an affirmative ring. Shalom implies unity, wholeness, completeness, fullness—all positive terms. Shanti, the Hindu counterpart, denotes spiritual contentment, a profound integration of one's inner life.

In catechism classes children learn of hell, purgatory, and heaven.

War is hell. Man is sinful. The strategy, then, is to appeal to people out of fear. The tablet Moses received commands readers to refrain from murder. Those who disobey face the weeping and gnashing of teeth. More and more weapons are produced to serve as a deterrent to war. Hiroshima reminds mortals of the prospect of mutual assured destruction for which the acronym MAD has been coined. Yet this strategy seems practical, as a half-century has passed since an atomic bomb has been dropped in battle. Margaret Thatcher contends the costly arms build-up during the '80s was worth every penny spent. The Cold War petered out with nary a shot.

Limbo takes on the aspect of the lull, a retreat for partisans of peaceful coexistence. As Pope John avers, negotiating is preferable to fighting.

When the wise convened to ruminate over the 1963 papal encyclical, Nehru spoke up: "What is needed is a zeal and passion for civilized behavior in international affairs." Lasting peace cannot be based on fear alone. He continued, "We must make peace a more positive, dynamic, and exciting idea."

The Ways to Peace

The idea takes several forms. Bishop Walter Sullivan of the Catholic Diocese in Richmond, Virginia, served in 1993 as the president of Pax Christi in the United States. In conversation, he spoke of the cry for justice, which leads to peace. He thought Americans tended to associate peace with security and the protection of material possessions rather than with justice. He recalled the development of the people of Israel. He remarked, "They were faithful to God. Out of the notion of shalom comes the whole being, reconciliation, and healing. Walk humbly with God." He alluded to passages in Isaiah and Micah. He added, "And we should look to Jesus and how He lived. The Gospel holds for non-violence, and Jesus shows what it is to be God-like."

Conflict resolution offers one avenue. People recognize that intolerance exists. Folks divide into groups, and the "us" versus "them" mentality sets in. A Randolph-Macon College psychologist, Dr. Michael Wessels, observed that the "first thing you do in creating an enemy image is you strip away all human characteristics. Then, if you can make him a pest, it actually becomes beneficial to kill him." So the Japanese in World War II were deemed simply subhuman. In the eyes of one American cartoonist, they were *head lice* whose *breeding grounds* needed to be annihilated. A Japanese cartoonist compared Americans with a case of dandruff to be scraped from the pure, chaste head of Japan.

Wessels saw a similar perspective in the Middle East. "The Jordanians are rats," a Palestinian refugee in Jordan snarled. "You can't deal with them as people." Later the psychologist overheard a group of Israel settlers commenting, "The Palestinians are animals."

As Confucius wrote, investigate and shatter enemy images through education. In *Arab and Jew*, a Pulitzer Prize winner,

David Shipler, devoted the major portion of the text to the division of the two peoples and then quoted a teacher near the end: "It all comes down to shaping one individual at a time." Acquainting oneself with the land of Nehru not only obliterates the "them" concept but offers insight into the stance towards peace in the Indian tradition. The Hindu approach to peace traces violence to thoughts and desires which are stressful. Meditation removes stress from the nervous system. The person then becomes peaceful. When one percent of a community meditates in consort, the environment is positively affected.

The devotion to the resolving of conflict promotes communication, which overcomes prejudice. A participant in a peace dialogue wrote of his own tendency to spout words without thought. When he replied,

> 'Yes, but...' I am generally, in thought or speech, discarding that to which my yes refers and announcing my disagreement. And I am admitting that I have stopped my listening. And I am risking a confusion in my ongoing learning process.

Other avenues offer promise. Charles Walton, a California resident, sponsored a contest for an essay on peace among students. He donated $1,600 for prizes. Some remarks on prejudice and intolerance cited previously were taken from the winner, a high school senior. Alfred Nobel endowed a fund to honor a citizen or cause annually for the promotion of peace. Peace enthusiasts in America advocate the establishment of an academy on the model of West Point to develop a curriculum for the teaching of peace.

The commitment to the cause through education, tolerance, and communication with people from other cultures and traditions may be salutary for Americans, as violence is more rampant in the United States. Pfaff and Stillman in *The Politics of Hysteria* stated that cases of total war by non-

Western societies are rare; elsewhere battles are limited to clearly defined ends.

The proscription against killing was the Sixth Commandment received by Moses. More commanding are the first two prescribing love, the unifying force. Arms are for hugging. Fear deters the descent to hell; love leads to the peace that passeth understanding.

Who is Responsible for Peace? The U.N.? You?

So where does peace start? With you? With world government? Confucius deliberated on the question centuries ago. Those who shudder at the prospect of a nuclear Armageddon start with a political construct. Statesmen sought to develop weapons to make war impossible. The species would survive, as sane leaders would never deliberately wipe out civilization. But what about a conflagration by chance as speculated by Pope John in *Pacem in Terris*?

World government is the only way, said one participant in the colloquium meeting to discuss the Pope's encyclical, which acknowledged that states have the right to exist. The nation-state, according to a French minister, had been made obsolete by the nuclear revolution. Herman Kahn agreed in commenting that even a bad world government might be better than no world government. The overall sentiments, though, of those gathered were more in accord with the Pope.

Quoting Pope Pius XII, "Nothing is lost by peace; everything may be lost by war," Pope John urged the creation of a worldwide authority empowered to act from consent rather than force. He urged a balanced reciprocal reduction in armaments, and he endorsed the declarations of the United Nations. In the initial articles of the first chapter of the Charter, the purposes of the United Nations were outlined:

1. To maintain international peace and security, and to that end: to take effective collective measures for the prevention and removal of threats to the peace, and the suppression of acts of aggression or other breaches of peace, and to bring about by peaceful means, and in conformity with the principles of justice and international law, adjustment or settlement of international disputes or situations which might lead to a breach of the peace;

2. To develop friendly relations among nations based on self-respect for the principles of equal rights and self-determination of peoples, and to take other appropriate measures to strengthen universal peace.

Pope John stated that the framework had become defective by the date of the publication of the encyclical almost two decades later. But with the 1990s thaw between the members of the Security Council, the UN can now fulfill its purposes.

History evidences that nations will insist on their right to exist. In Kant's essay entitled "Eternal Peace," he traced in 1795 the rampant militarism in Europe to its expansion into America, Africa, and Asia.

> If we compare the barbarian instances of inhospitality... with the inhuman behavior of the civilized, and especially the commercial, states of our continent, the injustice practiced by them even in their first contact with foreign lands and peoples fills us with horror; the mere visiting of such peoples being regarded by them as equivalent to a conquest. America, the Negro lands... on being discovered were treated as countries that belonged to nobody; for the aboriginal inhabitants were reckoned as nothing.

Americans objected and insisted on sovereignty. We are reluctant to cede that power to others today. One person remarked at the 1965 papal colloquium, "If U Thant's suggestion of throwing the Cuban missile crisis into the UN had been accepted, I think the missiles would still be in Cuba."

Other countries feel likewise. Pfaff asserted that all Africa and Asia give witness to the sociological and psychological devastation left by three centuries of European rule. Muhammed Khan, judge of the International Court of Justice, also spoke at the convention responding to the Pope:

> The emphasis on nationalism and insistence upon national sovereignty have been intensified as an aftermath of the colonial system. Peoples who have been under domination are sensitive on anything that touches sovereignty.

National independence, the sense of one's own nationhood, must be the basis of any kind of reasonable world order.

The Community as the Center

If not the nation, then look to the community to build peace. Peace starts there in the mind of Scott Peck, author of *The Distant Drum*. Peck believes the greatest deterrent to stopping the arms race is passivity. Helplessness confronts the mortal in considering his role to create peace at the world level. Overcome inertia; get active; build community. The rules for community-making and peace-making are identical. In a community, differences are both celebrated and acknowledged—but also transcended.

Communities have cropped up at all levels. Citizens in Vermont started a coalition of 50 groups to establish the US-USSR Bridges for Peace program in 1983. The participants aimed to challenge deeply rooted "enemy images." In the improved climate that followed, "bridges" began to foster cooperative activities through publications, religious exchanges, and tours. In another example, Atlanta, Georgia, serves as the home base for The Friendship Force, which stresses "faces, not places." Its mission statement follows:

> By joining the Friendship Force as a Host or Ambassador, I understand that I am embarking on an important personal mission. That mission is to befriend strangers, whether at home or abroad. My new friends and I can make a difference. A world of friends will be a world of peace.

Men and women in cities and towns across the country have established peace education centers that carry out the community-building Peck advocates. In Richmond, Virginia, a three-member staff, working out of offices provided gratis by the Catholic Diocese with a $65,000 annual budget raised from the community, has introduced an Alternative for Violence project in two prisons. Now into its 13th year, the Richmond Peace Education Center also collaborates with elementary schools in teaching children how to mediate conflicts.

The Family as the Center

Peace can begin with a smaller unit, the family. The recipient of a Medal of Honor by the United Nations Society of Writers in 1992 claimed women hold the key, because the values they instill in their children will determine the way those children will treat others. Child-rearing, the honoree affirmed, should not be devalued, as it is the very root of any future world peace.

Women carry their fetuses for nine months and then experience the pains of labor. They then nurture the child. In the process, they become life preservers. In *Maternal Thinking*, Sara Riddick pointed out that the aim toward peace is not just a graceful gift that women develop as mothers, but the very practice of motherhood fosters life preservation.

Moreover, through observation, the father can absorb and apply those lessons in nurturing.

Jean Flores, a single mother and editor of *Peace Notes*, observed her ten-year-old son fascinated by guns. Violence is a staple of television programs for children. Duty impels parents to monitor the books and television fare to which their children are exposed. Ultimately, too, the extent to which the mother and father can live together in concord has an extraordinary effect on the child. The behavior of father and mother toward one another sets an example for the resolution of conflict to the child. And the parents are inextricably bound to every youngster's and thereafter adult's quest for personal peace.

Moses received Ten Commandments. Alcoholics Anonymous adherents prescribe a 12-step course for the addict. How about a 12-rung ladder to peace?

Peace Starts With You

1. Forgive yourself and ask forgiveness of others. God will help. As Alan Paton avers, "It is essential that we ask for forgiveness; otherwise, we shall not recognize or experience it." You have one person to live with for the balance of your life: yourself. Ask for forgiveness and put the sins of the past behind you.

I stole candy from the corner store as an eighth grader. More than two decades later, I wrote the store owner, apologized, and made restitution (yes, with interest). Now I can enter that business and greet the proprietor with a clear conscience.

2. Forgive others. You cannot hope to be an instrument of peace when you are not at peace with others.

3. *Expose yourself to works that show that war is hell and peace is good.* Reality must be encountered. The movies *Breaker Morant, Casualties of War*, and *Gallipoli* show the absurdity of combat. Novels such as *The Red Badge of Courage* and *All Quiet on the Western Front* do likewise. The human toll from war is terrible as an anonymous poet reminds readers:

Who will fire the cannons
When the ones who fought have died
When the corpses all lie rotting
And the crimson flood has dried

When the children huddle weeping
Sickened by the stench
Of the muddy, bloody soldiers
Lying bloated in the trench

Will the hollow songs of mourning
Haunt a bleak and barren land
As we place the clean white crosses
Over fresh heaped mounds of sand

Or will we claim a victory
As we tally up the score
And wait with patriotic zeal
For the next Great War?

Then read Paton's *Instrument of Thy Peace* or Knowles' *A Separate Peace* for a redemptive view of reconciliation.

4. *Tolerate skepticism.* History shows that peaceful times have only been interludes. The omnipresence of sin and evil warrant a pragmatic attitude. To paraphrase Paul in the New Testament, "I believe in peace; help my unbelief."

5. *Respect the role of humor.* Laughter deflects anger and waylays aggressive instincts. Emily Nghiem recited her poem at Rice University:

FEDERAL EXPRESSION

An Urgent Message to the White House

You said to make a sacrifice,
So Griffin shot a doctor thrice.
[3 squirts]:
ANTI-Life!
ANTI-God!
ANTI-Christ or Christian Fraud!
You said it's time to stop the blame,
but who can stop the Crying Game?
[4 squirts]:
Cries for FREEDOM! Human RIGHTS!
MOTHER EARTH and JESUS CHRIST!
[Random squirts]:
RELIGIONS! RIFLES!! What a mixture!!!
(The Bill of RIGHTS and BIBLE SCRIPTURE?)
You said it's time to make a change:
Put more Policemen on the range!
But load 'em up with WATER GUNS -
(All "Civil War" should be this fun!)

(Performed with a fully loaded water gun, preferably a SUPER SOAKER)

6. *Pay attention and be alert to the "symptoms of inner peace."* A subscriber to Peace Notes, Vicky Rovere, submitted a contribution. She wrote, "Be on the lookout. The hearts of a great many have already been exposed to inner peace, and it is possible that people everywhere could come down with it in epic proportions."

Ms. Rovere lists some signs of inner peace:

- A tendency to think and act spontaneously rather than on fears based on past experience.

- An unmistakable ability to enjoy each moment.
- A loss of interest in judging other people.
- A loss of interest in interpreting the actions of others.
- A loss of interest in conflict.
- A loss of the ability to worry. (She calls this serious.)
- Frequent, overwhelming episodes of appreciation.
- Contented feelings of connectedness with others and nature.
- Frequent attacks of smiling.
- An increasing tendency to let things happen rather than make them happen.
- An increased susceptibility to the love extended by others as well as the uncontrollable urge to extend it.

7. *Honor and support those who work for peace.* Pope John in *Pacem in Terris* suggested that men and women express appreciation to those who restore relations. Nobel took this course in the establishment of a prize to people and organizations engaged in the cause.

8. *Recognize the difference between the sexes.* Women carry less testosterone in their systems. They hold and nurse babies at their breast. Mothers as mothers become peacemakers. Margaret Mead and Pearl Buck have both written of the difference of the behavior of the two sexes in other cultures. Men are trained to fight. Therefore, these writers urge that women participate and vote at the war table. Women have special talents as negotiators. And they suffer the most in wars—losing husbands, sons, and homes.

9. *Communicate with a possible adversary.* In the midst of the Cold War, Americans and Russians became pen pals. The

play "A Walk in the Woods" portrayed the human dimension at work between two negotiators. In a take-off on a spiritual, a restaurateur recommended the recipe, "Let's bake bread together." The woman, founder of the Peace Table, brought hundreds of chefs—Palestinians and Jews, Russians and Americans—together in kitchens and at dinner tables.

10. Meditate on peace. Think about the implications of these passages from Scripture.

Isaiah 2:4: *"And he shall judge among the nations, and shall rebuke many people; and they shall beat their swords into plowshares, and their spears into pruning hooks: nation shall not lift up sword against nation, neither shall they learn war any more."*

Matthew 5:9: *"Blessed are the peacemakers: for they shall be called the children of God."*

Philippians 4:8: *"Finally, brethren, whatsoever things are true, whatsoever things are honest, whatsoever things are just, whatsoever things are pure, whatsoever things are lovely, whatsoever things are of good report; if there be any virtue, and if there be any praise, think on these things... and the peace of God shall be with you."*

Believers in the Hindu faith and adherents to the transcendental meditation theory of collective consciousness hold that if one percent of a people meditate, negative tendencies in society decline.

11. Pray. The Reverend Benjamin Campbell, pastoral director of Richmond Hill, an ecumenical retreat center in Richmond, wrote of two prayers for peace.

> Prayer for peace is the most fundamental prayer of the human being. Many of us are being drawn now to pray for peace, in ways that we do not completely understand. This is as it should be. In a sense, all true prayer precedes understanding. We find ourselves doing something that seems like praying, and then we wonder why we are doing it, what we

are supposed to be doing, how we are supposed to do it, and what we are to expect from it. The first prayer for peace is the individual, quiet search for peace. Whenever any person seeks for the peace of God within, that person becomes a seed of peace in the world.

Our peace within, whenever found, is recognized as a place where no bitterness, rage, or jealousy can take root—a place on which clear and clean judgment can be based. It is the place in which true reform begins.

The reformation of the world is necessary in order for true peace to exist, for there is no peace without justice. When you seek peace within, you invite God to begin the reformation of the world by reforming you.

The second prayer for peace is intercessory prayer. As the Lord gives us information through experience, through conversation, through imagination and speculation, or through news reports, our hearts are moved. That movement may take the form of anxiety. We may feel a desire to forget what we feel, or we may be pleased or angered or saddened by it. What we do not realize is that this movement in the soul is meant to be an invitation to prayer.

When we pray about specific persons and situations, we offer to God our thoughts, our thoughts about our thoughts, our hopes, our wishes, and our feelings—especially those feelings and pictures which are beyond words. We offer these thoughts and feelings for His healing and peace.

In a separate column, Campbell wrote that he liked the style of General H. Norman Schwarzkopf. The general had closed an interview with David Frost stating that he aspired to live his life in the spirit of St. Francis of Assisi, who prayed,

Lord, make me an instrument of Thy peace.
Where there is hatred, let me sow love;
Where there is injury, pardon;
Where there is doubt, faith;

Where there is despair, hope;
Where there is sadness, joy;
Where there is darkness, light.

12. *Work for peace.* Loving and warring cannot coexist. One must take precedence over the other. Prayer, friends, and meditation may incite you to consider a peaceful act. Follow through. Go for it!

Let there be peace on earth and let it begin with me (and you).

On Freedom

"We hold these truths to be self-evident, that all men are created equal, that they are endowed by their Creator with certain inalienable rights, that among these are Life, Liberty, and the Pursuit of Happiness."

DECLARATION OF INDEPENDENCE—JULY 4, 1776

"We the people of the United States, in order to form a more perfect Union, establish Justice, insure domestic Tranquility, provide for the common Defence, promote the general Welfare, and secure the Blessings of Liberty to ourselves and our posterity, do ordain and establish this Constitution for the United States of America."

PREAMBLE TO THE CONSTITUTION OF THE UNITED STATES

The nation's first president served with distinction. In his honor, the Congress proposed that George Washington's head be stamped on a new coin. Dissenters warned of future Neros and Caesars. In the end, the coin was adorned with the female figure of Liberty.

How could Thomas Jefferson announce that God, Who gives life, gives liberty at the same time? The proclamation arises from a view of nature. A person is born free. In 1690, John Locke had written two treatises on civil government. He declared that to be at liberty is to be at one with nature.

Freedom can be ceded only with personal consent. Otherwise, nature is violated. He stated,

> To understand political power aright… we must consider what estate all men are naturally in, and that is a state of perfect freedom to order their actions and dispose of their possessions and persons as they think fit within the bounds of the law of Nature without asking leave or depending upon the will of another man.

A Question of Nature

He continued, "This freedom from absolute, arbitrary power is so necessary to and closely joined with a man's preservation, that he cannot part with it but by what forfeits his preservation and life altogether." The idea that freedom can be given to a person is a widely held misconception. On the contrary, all individuals have freedom at birth; it can only be *given* to them after it has first been taken away by some governing authority. Responding to a claim that freedom is a basic need to be conferred at birth, a libertarian, Jorj Strumolo of Warwick, Rhode Island, asserted that since freedom is inborn, rather than the inclination toward it, there can be no possibility of an outside power having to allow it.

An immigrant from Romania explained his coming to America in 1983. Vivi Boborodeo, now a medical doctor, came to the United States at 14. "Freedom is more than the right to travel, to speak at will, to choose professions. It is a state of being," he said.

Seminal minds that have reflected on the nature of freedom have compared a man with another living organism, the tree. Henry Thoreau writing his classic, *Civil Disobedience*, noted that "when an acorn and a chestnut fall side by side...both obey their own laws and spring and grow and nurture as best they can, till one, perchance, overshadows and destroys the other. If a plant cannot live according to its own nature, it dies; and so a man."

Less than a decade later, John Stuart Mill followed with a thesis on liberty. Human nature, like the tree, grows and develops according to inner vital forces. The individual should be wary about tampering with the tree. Yes, sometimes liberty can degenerate into licentiousness. James Madison, the author of the Bill of Rights, exalted the liberty of the press. He expressed concern over excess and abuse. He said, "This licentiousness is an evil inseparable from the good with which it is allied" ... yet "perhaps it is a shoot which cannot be stripped from the stalk without wounding vitally the plant from which it is torn."

In the *Story of Philosophy*, Will Durant reviewed a 17th century political treatise penned by Spinoza prior to Locke's publication. Durant paraphrased the aim of the government, "Freedom is the goal of the state because the function of the state is to promote growth." In the Tractus Politicus, Spinoza had claimed,

> *The last end of the state is not to dominate men, nor to restrain them by fear; rather it is so to free each man from fear that he may live and act with full security and without injury to himself or his neighbor. The end of the state, I repeat, is not to make rational beings into brute beasts and machines. It is to enable their bodies and their minds to function safely. It is to lead men to live by, and to exercise, a free reason; that they may not waste their strength in hatred, anger, and guile, nor act unfairly toward one another. Thus the end of the state is really liberty.*

The libertarian in the 20th century would amend the last sentence and change the word *is* to *ought to be*. A devotee to the cause, Ardell L. Taylor of Patagonia, Arizona, wrote, "The end of the state ought really to be liberty, because obviously, under present conditions, it isn't."

Spinoza's idea of individual freedom holds true today. Man was not born to be forced but to breathe after his own fashion. Paul Munson, a partner in Kanawha Capital Management, Inc., a Richmond, Virginia asset management firm, has commented at length on contemporary developments in Eastern Europe in newsletters and luncheon addresses. In an interview in his living room, he said, "For all of human history, mankind has been making an effort toward freedom. A typical individual seeks freedom from another person to be overbearing—in telling him what to eat, when to sleep." He deemed the quest for freedom instinctive. Americans don't like authority. The quest has been intertwined with the nation's heritage. He linked capitalism to economic freedom, which was attuned to man's nature in providing an incentive for risk and hard labor.

An Ultimate Benefit

A law school dean ranked Mill's *On Liberty* with the Social Contract and Communist Manifesto as a lode for political and social theory for the western world. Mill favored liberty because the presence of freedom promoted the search for and revelation of the truth through the unfettered exchange of ideas.

The truth will out when any voice can vent itself in the marketplace of ideas. The presence of a diversity of opinion is vital to the pursuit of truth. Mill wrote, "The only way in which a human being can make some approach to knowing the whole of a subject is by hearing what can be said about it by persons of every variety of opinion and studying all modes in which it can be looked at by every character of mind." The exercise of reason will distinguish truth from falsehood.

"The peculiar evil of silencing the expression of an opinion is that it is robbing the human race," Mill wrote. For man is consequently deprived of the opportunity to exchange truth for error. All silencing of discussion is an assumption of infallibility. Ages are no more infallible than individuals. Thus if the choice were having a government or newspapers, Jefferson would have selected the latter.

Justice Oliver Wendell Holmes, in an opinion for the Supreme Court, declared that people realized that time had upset many faiths once fiercely held. And they have come to believe

> ... that the ultimate goal desired is better reached by the free trade of ideas—that the best test of truth is the power of the thought to get itself accepted in the competition of the market, and that the truth is the only ground upon which their (the people's) wishes safely can be carried out. That, at any rate, is the theory of our Constitution.

Freedom is a given in America. But it might be otherwise. Alexis De Toqueville wrote *Democracy in America* in 1831 five years after a tour of the United States. He noted,

> The Anglo-American relies upon personal interest to accomplish his ends and gives free scope to the unguided strength and common sense of the people; the Russian centres all the authority of society in a single arm. The principal instrument of the former is freedom; of the latter, servitude. Their starting point is different, and their courses are not the same; yet each of them seems marked by the Will of Heaven to sway the destinies of half the globe.

The Foe — Equality

"I have sought to point out the dangers to which the principle of equality exposes the independence of man," wrote

De Toqueville. What are those dangers? The people elect their own guardians. They choose legislators who take equality for their first principle and watchword. Government leaders do so much that the exercise of free will among the people becomes less useful and frequent. The people become a flock of timid animals for which government is the shepherd.

Why the preference for equality to freedom? For De Toqueville the answer lay in the human heart, which harbored a depraved taste that impels the weak to lower the powerful to their own level and prompts men to elect equality in slavery to inequality with freedom. He observed, "Not that those nations whose social condition is democratic naturally despise liberty; on the contrary, they have an instinctive love for it. But liberty is not the chief and constant object of their desires; equality is their idol." Later and again, "Democratic communities have a natural taste for freedom, but for equality their passion is ardent and insatiable."

Liberty requires exertion and sacrifice. Equality does not. The advantages of freedom are shown through the lapse of time. The benefits of equality are immediate and nothing is "required but to live." De Toqueville wrote, "Political liberty bestows exalted pleasures, from time to time, upon a certain number of citizens. Equality every day confers a number of small enjoyments on every man. The charms of equality are instantly felt."

Nobel Prize winner Friedrich von Hayek quoted De Toqueville in distinguishing democracy from socialism. They share a word in common—equality. The former seeks equality in liberty; the latter in restraint and servitude. Socialism presumes that for a man to be free "the despotism of physical want" has to be broken. The idea ultimately constitutes a claim for the equal distribution of wealth. Government embarks upon planning for the sake of justice. Thereafter it cannot refuse responsibility for anyone's fate or position. A government that undertakes to direct economic activity will necessarily use its power to realize somebody's ideal of distributive justice. Hayek prefers the individualist tradition that created Western civilization. At the outset of *The Road to Serfdom* he explained that he intends "to release the creative energy of individuals rather than devise a machinery for 'guiding' or 'directing' them."

Will and Ariel Durant summed up the experience of three millennia. "Nature smiles at the union of freedom and equality in our utopias. For freedom and equality are sworn and everlasting enemies, and when one prevails the other dies." In their final book of an eleven volume series entitled *The Story of Civilization*, they concluded that the hostile hungers had taken their turn in dominating the history of modern man. "The hunger for liberty, to the detriment of equality, was the recurrent theme of the 19th century in Europe and America; the hunger for equality, at the cost of liberty, has been the dominant aspect of European and American history in the 20th century." The dismantling of the Soviet Union near the end of this century presages a turn to liberty throughout the globe.

The Locus of Power

The battle between freedom and equality is fought in defining the role of government. Where does power lie? Henry Thoreau answered that question when he asserted, "There will never be a really free and enlightened state until the State comes to recognize the individual as a higher and independent power from which all its power and authority are derived and treats him accordingly." Everyman is a king seated on his throne. Yet he rules only one subject—himself.

Thoreau traced the historic progress of a political entity from an absolute to a limited monarchy and then to a democracy—an ascent toward the true respect for an individual. Locke had earlier expressed similar sentiments. "I should have a liberty to follow my own will in all things where that will prescribes ... and not to be subject to the inconstant, unknown arbitrary rule of man."

In the collectivist state, the rights of society supersede those of the individual. Ends are more important than means. Certain virtues, self-reliance and an acute moral sense, ebb. When the state tells the citizen to whom he can rent an apartment there is an implication of a grown adult being told how to behave. That is a form of disrespect, as the American is deprived of the right to form his own opinion, even if it is wrong. Hayek spoke of a man's responsibility to his conscience and the awareness of duty not exacted by compulsion. Man should be confronted by "the necessity to decide which of the things one values are to be sacrificed to others and to bear the consequences of one's decision—the very essence of any morals which deserve the name."

Father may not know best; Big Brother, to the contrary, needs to know only what he is told. The late Sidney Morton, an inveterate letter-to-the-editor writer and one time Sunday *Parade Magazine* contributor, spoke heatedly,

> I resent the government telling me what to do. I like to do what I want to do and have the right to do if it harms no one else. Homeowners no longer have the freedom to choose the tenants to whom they rent rooms or apartments, except within narrow limits, and here I am thinking more about the loss of freedom of association than about the economic and financial relationships.

The state acts only with the person's consent.

Thomas Jefferson said, "That government is best which

governs least," which Thoreau amended to, "That government is best which governs not at all." Government never itself furthered any enterprise but by the alacrity with which it got out of its way.

So Americans responded enthusiastically when they heard Ronald Reagan warm up an audience with the statement, "Government is not the solution to our problem; government is the problem." For a libertarian, government is a necessary evil which must be firmly chained lest it ravage one's rights. Americans have a healthy suspicion of power. They limit the number of days state legislatures can meet in session. One skeptic inquired, "What if all the voting and studying up for voting only took an hour or so a week as seems reasonable for a bare minimum-sized government?"

The authors (Jay, Madison, and Hamilton) of the Federalist papers, designed to explain and promote the adoption of the Constitution, were concerned about the abuses of both power and liberty. If every word of the Constitution decided a question between power and liberty, in the end government had to have, to Madison's mind, enough power—just enough—to carry out its main task, the protection of liberty and property. Thus in the democratic experiment that has now survived more than two centuries, the Constitution's founders deliberately prevented the concentration of power by separating—through an intricate system of checks and balances—legislative, executive, and judicial functions.

Role of Government

Jay C. Wood, a minarchist by self-definition, served as the editor of a libertarian newsletter. In response to a query, he listed the three legitimate functions of government: to provide (1) for the common defense from outside aggression, (2) a domestic police force for inside aggressors, and (3) an impartial court system to air and resolve grievances.

James Madison in his first inaugural address identified an armed and trained militia as the firmest bulwark of republics. Government, too, acts to prevent one person from harming others and, conversely, to protect one from harm by others. Locke claimed that aim served as the genesis of political societies. The citizen is free to do everything that injures no one else; but when one becomes a nuisance to others, society properly intervenes.

Adam Smith also speculated on the role of government. He listed three functions in *The Wealth of Nations*. The first two conformed to the Jay Wood thesis, but the third ceded to the government "certain public works and certain public institutions, which it can never be for the interest of any individual, or small number of individuals, to erect and maintain." Others have seen the judiciary as a defender of individual liberty rather than the locus for the resolution of disputes implied by Wood's litany. (Editorial note; if Peggy Noonan, President Reagan's speech-writer, had asked the author to collaborate, justice would have been added to the presidential litany in the preface and received a chapter in this book.)

Virtue of Competition

Ever since the founding fathers wrote the instruments that have guided the nation, Americans have learned from experience that there must be "options" to be free. Those in deliberation 200 years ago abhorred political parties. Nor were they aware that leviathans would form monopolies to restrain trade. So government properly intercedes to see that a choice exists.

In politics the choice is made on Election Day. Paul Munson of Richmond, Virginia said, "We need to live in a two party system where leaders are held accountable and can be unseated. Voting gives me the chance to replace poor leaders." The groundswell for term limits reflects the voter's view that incumbents have unfair advantages, such as franking privileges, in facing opponents.

And competition makes variety, not losers. Hayek deemed freedom in economic affairs an unforeseen by-product of political freedom. The presence of competing products dispenses with any mandate for "conscious social control."

The creation of wealth, too, has been a by-product of a competitive society with voluntary association in the private sector. A French physiocrat, Gournay, who served in the Bureau of Commerce in Paris, expressed his views (1759) after witnessing the restraints put by guild and governmental regulations upon economic enterprise. Economic rules should be reduced as "every man knows better than the government what procedure best favors his work; when each man is free to follow his interest more goods will be produced, wealth will grow." Two centuries later in *Wealth and Poverty*, George Gilder attributed this prosperity to the phenomenon of self-transcendence. Man rises above himself and, in so doing, creates wealth.

James Madison deemed conscience the most sacred of all property. He was religious. As President of the United States, he commended days of prayer and thanksgiving. He was pleased that different congregations found adherents in America. "A variety of sects is the best and only security for religious liberty in any society—for where such a variety exists, there cannot be a majority for any one sect to oppress and persecute the rest."

Bill of Rights

During the ratification of the Constitution, national leaders promised to draft an addendum to promote and preserve individual rights. James Madison, a congressman from Virginia in the initial session of the U.S. House of Representatives, became the principal working architect of those rights.

Madison explained the role of such personal guarantees in popular government. He wrote,

> The political truths declared in that solemn manner acquire by degrees the character of fundamental maxims of free government, and, as they become incorporated with the national sentiment, counteract the impulses of interest and passion.

The private citizen deserved safeguards against impulsive legislatures, arbitrary executives, and thoughtless popular majorities. The government could oppress. But the greatest danger to liberty lay "in the body of the people, operating by the majority against the minority." Such a majority might favor—in the name of equality—the confiscation of property. Against that majority the prescriptions of liberty should be leveled.

If a Bill of Rights were added to the Constitution, "independent tribunals of justice will consider themselves in a peculiar manner the guardian of those rights." The courts would provide an impenetrable bulwark against federal invasion by the legislature and executive.

In 1789, Madison prepared an outline for the Bill of Rights and looked to many sources. He gleaned the deliberations of state conventions during ratification. He searched through the eight state constitutions containing bills of rights to find half of the proposals he suggested. He reviewed the 20 libertarian proposals crafted by George Mason for the Virginia

Convention of 1788 and steeped himself in the history of Great Britain from the Magna Carta onwards.

"A man has property in his opinions and the free communication of them," Madison wrote. In reading history he found that freedom of religion was rarely realized. In England, jurors had been imprisoned for disobeying the court's orders to convict two Quakers, William Penn and a friend. The Anglican Church had been officially established in Virginia. Patrick Henry introduced a bill in the Virginia legislature in 1784 containing a provision for teachers of the Christian religion.

Thomas Jefferson drafted the first legislation in the history of mankind to outlaw religious persecution. He inserted two clauses—one to prohibit the establishment of any religion, and the second to guarantee the free exercise of any belief. Jefferson wrote his epitaph: "Here was buried Thomas Jefferson, author of the Declaration of American Independence, of the Statute of Virginia for religious freedom, and the father of the University of Virginia." The Statute creating the hallowed wall of separation of church and state was passed by the Virginia Assembly in 1786. Madison had shepherded the bill through while Jefferson served as ambassador in France.

Madison then proceeded to incorporate these two freedoms—the freedom from any state-endorsed religion and the freedom of religion—in the First Amendment of the Constitution.

America's Original Blight

The Bill of Rights did not at the outset embrace all Americans. The first amendments did not encompass certain black people—slaves. John Locke expressed his thoughts on slavery and natural liberty in 1690. He wrote,

> Slavery is so vile and miserable an estate of man, and so directly opposite to the generous temper and courage of our nation that it is hardly to be conceived that 'an Englishman, much less a gentleman,' should plead for it.

Yet Americans did plead for that miserable estate. Civil rights had been left to the states. The cancer led to Henry Thoreau's classic 1849 essay *Civil Disobedience* and an endorsement of Madison's proposition that the conscience is the most sacred of all property.

Henry Thoreau believed that an honest man revolted when his conscience was violated. For the conscience of a citizen transcended the power of the state. Thoreau lamented the practice of slavery. Rebellion was in order. Opponents of reform in his native Massachusetts were more interested in commerce and agriculture than the plight of the slave. Others wailed with their hands in their pockets. They could do more.

For Thoreau, the effective means to revolt lay in refusing to pay taxes for the cause he opposed. The essential revolution comes from acting on principle. That causes change. When unjust laws exist, the conscientious citizen either endeavors to amend them and obeys them until he succeeds or violates them at once. In any event, he "cannot lend himself to the wrong he condemns." Disobedience to an intolerable law leads to imprisonment. The jail then becomes the right place to be, as "under a government which imprisons any unjustly, the true place for a just man is also a prison," Thoreau asserted.

A minority is powerless while it conforms to the will of the majority. But as the minority fills up the cells in a protest against slavery, the State will "not hesitate to choose" between the just men and unjust cause. If a thousand men refuse to pay their taxes, a peaceful revolution will ensue. Thoreau brashly suggests to the conscientious objector that when confronted by the tax collector, he urge the officer to resign. The revolution will be accelerated.

Thoreau's message is enhanced by his own action as a man of principle. He wrote, "It costs me less in every sense to incur the penalty of disobedience to the State than it would be to obey." He refused to pay the poll tax. He went to jail. He reported, "I did not for a moment feel confined, and the walls seemed a great waste of stone and mortar. I felt as if I alone of all my townsmen had paid my tax." He was a free man in a jail where the jailers did not know how to treat him. The State has superior physical strength. It can resolve to punish the citizen's body. But not his intellect or moral senses.

The Dred Scott decision by the United States Supreme Court in 1857 affirmed that slaves were the property of others. "Gettysburg is the national shrine. The matter of personal rights was not settled until then. That battle meant that national government had the authority to act. The tide had turned," said commentator Munson. On January 1, 1863, Abraham Lincoln issued a proclamation, "All slaves in any states or area still in rebellion are declared free."

Following the Civil War the 14th Amendment was added to the Constitution guaranteeing civil rights for all citizens. No longer could the states abridge the rights declared in the earlier amendments.

While the battle may be over, skirmishes pop up. A century after the Emancipation Proclamation, Martin Luther King, Jr. wrote a letter from a Birmingham jail. He was responding to white clergymen criticizing him for "unwise and untimely" demonstrations. Like Thoreau—with a conscience oblivious to prison walls—he speculated on the need of the South, the nation, and the world for creative extremists:

> Before the Pilgrims landed at Plymouth, we were here. Before the pen of Jefferson etched across the pages of

history the majestic words of the Declaration of Independence, we were here. For more than two centuries, our foreparents labored in the country without wages; they made cotton 'king,' and they built the homes of their masters in the midst of brutal injustice and shameful humiliation—and yet out of a bottomless variety, they continued to thrive and develop. If the expressible cruelties of slavery could not stop us, the opposition we now face will surely fail. We will win our freedom because the sacred heritage of our nation and the eternal will of God are embodied in our echoing demands.

The Price

Former political prisoners are obsessed with human freedom. Adam Michnik saw his friends crushed about him in Poland in 1968. Years later he wrote a book while incarcerated. He said, "My whole personal experience is mostly the experience of defeat, of faithfulness to a defeated cause...I think only those causes are valuable for which you have to pay dearly. A freedom that doesn't cost much is not worth much... With all my heart, I support those students in Tiananmen Square. I believe that the blood they shed will not have been wasted. That kind of blood is never wasted."

Madison, Mill, and Thoreau all spoke of freedom as being as natural as the tree left to grow. "The tree of liberty must be refreshed from time to time with the blood of patriots and tyrants. It is its natural manure," wrote Thomas Jefferson two centuries before Michnik penned his thoughts.

Admiral James Stockdale spent seven years in a Hanoi prison during the Vietnamese War. He claimed that his appreciation for freedom stems from a first-hand understanding of its rarity. From his prison cell, he could hear the barking of loudspeakers on the street telling people what to think. An interrogator shouted at him, "We may not have freedom, but after 4000 years we have order, and we will settle for that."

Human freedom has not been the way of the world. In a 1980 *Parade Magazine* article celebrating Independence Day, Stockdale noted the asset—"our most precious national treasure"—was available only to a shrinking minority of people. After the nation's bitter struggle for independence, brave and earnest men stepped forward to write the Constitution. No one had to remind the Founding Fathers of the cost. Stockdale wrote,

> Fifty-six of them knowingly laid their lives, liberty, and honor on the line when they signed that Declaration of Independence. And they paid their dues. In the ensuing war, nine were killed in action, five died as prisoners of war, twelve had their homes burned, several lost sons, one man's wife died in prison, and seventeen (including Thomas Jefferson) went broke. Tom Paine summed up the legacy of these men very simply: 'Those who expect to reap the blessings of freedom must, like men, undergo the fatigue of supporting it.'

Patrick Henry provided the spark that fired the American experiment. On March 20, 1775, he spoke to those assembled at St. John's Church in Richmond:

> Three millions of people, armed in the holy cause of liberty, and in such a country as that which we possess, are invincible by any force which our enemy can send against us. Besides, sir, we shall not fight our battles alone. There is a just God who presides over the destinies of nations, and who will raise up friends to fight our battles for us. The battle, sir, is not to the strong alone; it is to the vigilant, the active, the brave. Besides, sir, we have no election. If we were base enough to desire it, it is now too late to retire from the contest. There is no retreat, but in submission and slavery! Our chains are forged, their clanking may be heard on the

plains of Boston! The war is inevitable—and let it come!! I repeat it, sir, let it come!!!

It is in vain, sir, to extenuate the matter. Gentlemen may cry, peace, peace—but there is no peace. The war is actually begun. The next gale that sweeps from the North will bring to our ears the clash of resounding arms! Our brethren are already in the field! Why stand we here idle? What is it that gentlemen wish? What would they have? Is life so dear, or peace so sweet, as to be purchased at the price of chains and slavery? Forbid it, Almighty God! I know not what course others may take; but as for me, give me liberty or give me death!

United States Bill Of Rights

Amendment 1. Congress shall make no law respecting an establishment of religion, or prohibiting the free exercise thereof; or abridging the freedom of speech, or of the press; or the right of the people peaceably to assemble, and to petition the government for a redress of grievances.

Amendment 2. A well-regulated militia being necessary to the security of a free State, the right of the people to keep and bear arms shall not be infringed.

Amendment 3. No soldier shall, in time of peace, be quartered in any house without the consent of the owner; nor in time of war but in a manner to be prescribed by law.

Amendment 4. The right of the people to be secure in their persons, houses, papers and effects, against unreasonable searches and seizures, shall not be violated, and no warrants shall issue but upon probable cause, supported by oath or affirmation, and particularly describing the place to be searched, and the persons or things to be seized.

Amendment 5. No person shall be held to answer for a capital or otherwise infamous crime, unless on a presentment or indictment of a grand jury, except in cases arising in the land or naval forces, or in the militia, when in actual service in time of war or public danger; nor shall any person be subject for the same offense to be twice put in jeopardy of life or limb; nor shall be compelled in any criminal case to be a witness against himself, nor be deprived of life, liberty, or property, without due process of law; nor shall private property be taken for public use, without just compensation.

Amendment 6. In all criminal prosecutions the accused shall enjoy the right to a speedy and public trial, by an impartial jury of the State and district wherein the crime shall have been committed, which district shall have been previously ascertained by law, and to be informed of the nature and cause of the accusation; to be confronted with the witnesses against him; to have compulsory process for obtaining witnesses in his favor, and to have the assistance of counsel for his defense.

Amendment 7. In suits at common law, where the value in controversy shall exceed twenty dollars, the right of trial by jury shall be preserved, and no fact tried by a jury shall be otherwise reexamined in any court of the United States than according to the rules of the common law.

Amendment 8. Excessive bail shall not be required, nor excessive fines imposed, nor cruel and unusual punishments inflicted.

Amendment 9. The enumeration in the Constitution of certain rights shall not be construed to deny or disparage others retained by the people.

Amendment 10. The powers not delegated to the United States by the Constitution, nor prohibited by it to the States, are reserved to the States respectively, or to the people.

On Work

"Fans, for the past two weeks you have been reading about a bad break I got. Yet today I consider myself the luckiest man on the face of the earth," said Lou Gehrig before 62,000 baseball fans on Lou Gehrig Appreciation Day—July 4, 1939. Shortly thereafter he died from the disease to which his name was given.

At the funeral the general manager of the New York Yankees, the team for which Gehrig had played, said, "Lou doesn't need tributes from anyone. His life and the way he lived were enough. He just went out and did his job every day."

Gehrig, the Iron Horse, played 2,151 straight games from 1925 to 1939 when the deteriorating disease crippled him and he announced to his manager, "I'm benching myself, Joe." During that span he established several records—23 grand slam home runs, the first in the 20th century to hit four home runs in one game, and an all time high of 184 RBIs in 1931 for an American Leaguer. But the record he is remembered for occurred when he eclipsed Everett Scott, who had played in 1307 consecutive games.

The author of *Iron Horse*, Ray Robinson, chose Gehrig over Babe Ruth as a subject; "I wanted my heroes to be less flamboyant, less outrageous, less self-centered, preferring the stubborn day-by-day dedication of Gehrig." Robinson wrote, "He was not a 'natural' in any sense of the word. Only grim determination to succeed plus his magnificent physique and stamina, had enabled him to make his way with the Yankees." Reporters noted Gehrig's ongoing pursuit to improve his game, especially as a fielder.

Robinson observed that durability has never been the most applause-winning ingredient in sport. But that essence captured the admiration of the biographer. Contrary to the remarks in his farewell address Gehrig did get some bad breaks. Every finger was broken during his career. One reporter recalled, "I can remember when he had a broken middle finger on his right hand. Every time he batted a ball it hurt him... You could see him wince. But he always stayed in the game."

Gehrig was asked how he endured. He replied, "I have the will to play."

Work and Survival

As a youth and but one of four children in his family to survive, Gehrig delivered laundry for his mother who toiled as a maid, taking in laundry from rich folks. His father had immigrated to America at 21 from his native Germany. The father, an art metal mechanic, pounded patterns into sheets of metal.

An article by Abraham Maslow outlining a hierarchy of human needs was published in 1943. Maslow defined survival through the consumption of food and water as the most elemental human need. America offered that promise to Gehrig's father who joined 6 million Germans, 5 million Italians, and 4.5 million Irish among the close to 40 million people who immigrated to America between 1820 and 1950.

Europe had been stricken by an insoluble agricultural crisis. Malthus predicted that the number of people would increase until subsistence was the lot of man. The gradual decline in the death rate among the newly born brought that forecast to reality. The increase in survival to adulthood strained the entire family; stability disappeared from peasant life. The steady recession in living standards led to a struggle for existence. Desperation prompted the massive departure.

Oscar Handlin, the historian, recounts in *The Uprooted* how peasants swarmed to European ports where they slept for a penny a night with as many as 40 packed into a 12-by-15 foot room. They then embarked, most in steerage, to spend 30 to 40 days at sea living in bunks on each side of a 5-foot aisle. The box-like spaces, 10' wide, 5' long, and 3' high, afforded housing for six to 10 people. Routinely one in 10 died at sea. The journey was shortened after 1840 with the advent of steam.

On arrival in America, the newcomers used picks and shovels to earn their daily bread. Unskilled laborers were needed to build canals, then lay 350,000 miles of railroad, establish 200,000 miles of highway, and thereafter construct city streets, trolley tracks, and gas pipes. They came to labor in whatever sector of the economy was expanding. The Germans came to the coalfield mines in Pennsylvania and thereafter to factories, as the availability of inexpensive labor converted production from a handicraft to a mechanized form of power.

The beginnings were hard. Not until the 1880's did a 10-hour limit on daily toil become a serious objective. In an appreciation of the nation's heritage, President Lyndon Baines Johnson triggered the renovation of Ellis Island in New York Harbor through which 12 million immigrants passed. A room has been dedicated—"At work in America." A poster on the wall tells an old Italian story, "Well, I came to America because I heard the streets were paved with gold. When I got here I found out three things; first, the streets weren't paved with gold; second, they weren't paved at all; and, third, I was expected to pave them."

Duty Calls

Historically the meaning of work has extended beyond mere survival. God calls. Rarely heard in the marketplace today is the notion that men and women diligently toil to fulfill their duty to God. Author Dorothy Sayers in *Creed or Chaos* put forth two propositions. First, "Work is not, primarily, a thing one does to live, but the thing one lives to do." It is the medium in which the worker offers himself to God and abides by His will. Secondly, "It is the business of the church to recognize that the secular vocation, as such, is sacred."

Work affects the soul profoundly. Thomas Moore reflected on his days as a novice in a religious order. As a fledgling monk, he was given the job of pruning trees. He wrote,

> I recall one day in particular.... It was a cold day in Wisconsin, and I was out on a limb sawing away at shoots sticking up on limbs all around me. I took a minute to rest, hoping the limb wouldn't suddenly break, and asked myself, 'Why am I doing this? I'm supposed to be learning prayer, meditation, Latin, and Gregorian chant. But here I am, my hands frostbitten, feeling not terribly secure in the top of a tree, my fingers bloody from an erratic saw blade, doing something I know nothing about.' The answer, I already knew, was that work is an important component of the spiritual life.... Monastic writers describe work as a path to holiness.

The fruits of toil lead to health and happiness—two interdependent elements in a good life. Research shows that job satisfaction retards aging. Every longevity study manifests that pleasure in one's work is the most reliable indicator that a person is at low risk for a heart attack. Both Aristotle and Jefferson have addressed the therapeutic aspects of work. The former said, "The essence of happiness is doing the best we can with the talents we have"; the latter, less directly in a letter to his daughters, "Of all the cankers of human happiness, none corrodes it with so silent, yet so baneful a tooth, as indolence."

The president of the Herman Miller Furniture Company in Texas addressed these sentiments in contemporary terms in *The Fifth Discipline*,

> Why can't work be one of the wonderful things in life? Why can't we cherish and praise it, versus seeing work as a necessity? Why can't it be a cornerstone in people's lifelong process of developing ethics, values, and in expressing the humanities and the arts? Why can't people learn through the process that there's something about the beauties of design, of building something to last, something of value? I believe that this potential is inherent in work, more so than in many other places.

Yet work is a necessity. The immigrants knew that. As man lives to pursue a call, he works to live. St. Paul declared, "The man who will not work shall not eat." And work supports the family. In America work provides the most effective anti-poverty program. Of workers with full-time, year-around jobs, less than three per cent have incomes below the poverty line.

What goes on at home is important, too. In the creation of a family, "labor" starts moments before birth and extends through delivery of the baby. Thereafter as anthologist William J. Bennett noted in the preface to the section on work in *The Book of Virtues*, labor continues as parents raise children. That task, though non-revenue producing, is essential to the health of each generation.

Beyond the family lies a community dependent on the common good and a sense of public duty. "A hundred times a day

I remind myself that my life depends on the labors of other men, living and dead, and that I must exert myself in order to give, in the measure I have received, and am still receiving," observed Albert Einstein, voicing his obligation to the community.

The community may have its own expectations as well. The federal government conducted a mathematics proficiency test among eighth-graders in the 40 states participating in the survey. North Dakota topped the rest, although it ranked 49th in teacher salaries. The superintendent sought to explain the results;

> The work ethic has to be at the front. When you're asked to do a job out here, and that includes going to school, you figure you have to get out there and do it. You just wouldn't think of leaving school here, and if you did, you'd have to explain it to a lot of people. It's parental involvement, but it's community involvement too. The community feels they own all their youngsters. If you're standing on a street corner in any town in North Dakota, people are going to come up and want to know what you are doing there.

God Toiled at the Beginning

God started it all. He created the world in six days and then took a day of rest to show there's more to life than a job. But at the outset, He showed that work is natural. For God worked. A man and a woman follow His lead in doing likewise.

Then God created Adam and put him in the Garden of Eden to till. The Reverend Thom Blair, an Episcopal priest, said, "God made man in His image. He intended that man work. It is in our nature. He gave Adam a garden to enjoy. Adam violated it, so work can be viewed as both aligned with human need and a burden, too."

Blair went on. He noted that the Jews believed in work.

When an important message was to be conveyed to King Saul, the messenger found him in the fields. Ben Franklin's father often repeated a proverb from Solomon to young men; "Seest thou a man diligent in his calling, he shall stand before kings."

The Greeks had led the Western world before Christ was born. The Greeks used slaves to perform menial chores. People of stature did not soil their hands, since paid employment degraded the mind. Rather they engaged in philosophical conversations.

Blair observed that Christ came as a teknon, the Greek term for an artisan who derives his livelihood from his hands. "He could have come as a head-knocker," Blair commented. Christ toiled as a carpenter, a vocation to make the yokes for oxen cited in Matthew's Gospel.

St. Paul followed the model as a tentmaker. Between travels he toiled to earn his sustenance. He wrote that he worked harder than others and urged those in Colossae: "Whatever you do, do it heartily, as if unto the Lord." Ultimately, according to scripture, the mortal is directed to behave so that on the day of reckoning he will be told, "Well done, good and faithful servant."

In the centuries that followed the idea resurfaced that some vocations were superior to others. The religious life—that of a monk or priest—commanded the greatest esteem and was sure to gain the most favor in the afterlife. Calvin and Luther dispelled that idea in asserting that the highest form of moral obligation of the individual lies in fulfilling mundane duties. No longer was the pursuit of an ordinary calling subordinate to ascetic aims. Work made God's love visible. Luther remarked, "A dairy maid can milk cows to the glory of God."

This view came ashore in America. As Sydney Ahlstrom chronicled in the *Religious History of the American People*, "Within a few years of the founding of the Massachusetts

Bay Colony in 1630, New England became the most exemplary, flowering place of Puritanism." The Puritan Ethic promulgated a concept of personal and public duty. Through a "call" man served God in some useful, productive occupation.

In the *Puritan Ethic and the American Revolution* Edmund S. Morgan declared,

> Before entering on a trade or profession, a man must determine whether he had a calling to undertake it. If he had talents for it, if it was useful to society, if it was appropriate to his station in life, he could feel confident that God called him to it. God called no one to a life of prayer or to a life of ease or to any life that added nothing to the common good.... Once called to an occupation, a man's duty to the Maker Who called him demanded that he labor assiduously at it. He must shun both idleness or neglect of his calling, and sloth, or slackness in it.... The emphasis throughout was on productivity for the benefit of society.

The Puritan ethic stressing diligence in the call also served to deter the laborer from sin, as work focused the mind on production. Gainful employment preserved morals and virtue. The American settlers sensed the sanctity of their daily pursuits. To work at one's calling led to the salvation of the soul.

This ethic was one of two elements in the rise of capitalism, according to Max Weber's classic, *The Protestant Ethic and the Spirit of Capitalism*, published in 1904. Industry and frugality caused a society built on capitalism to flourish. The success of a capitalistic society rested on a disciplined labor force and steady investment of financial resources.

The American Heritage

Weber, a German, quoted Ben Franklin time and again. Franklin coined maxims for publication in *Poor Richard's Almanac*; to wit, "The trade must be worked at and the calling well followed, and God gives all things to industry. Then plough deep, while sluggards sleep, and you shall have corn to sell and to keep."

Franklin as a minister in France in 1782 contrasted the European and American scenes. He wrote,

> Much less is it advisable for a person (emigrant) to go thither (America) who has no other quality to recommend him but his birth. In Europe it indeed has its value; but it is a commodity that can not be carried to a worse market than America, where people do not inquire concerning a stranger, "What is he?", but "What can he do?"

Franklin elaborated on this theme in noting,

> The people have a saying that God Almighty is himself a mechanic, the greatest in the universe, and he is respected and admired more for the variety, ingenuity, and utility of his handiwork than for the antiquity of his family.

One of Poor Richard's aphorisms held, "No man e'er was glorious who was not laborious."

In the following century the success ethic evidenced itself in the valor of Horatio Alger's heroes. Alger wrote tales of honesty triumphant. From 1860 to the turn of the century the stories, moving out of stores at a million copies a year pace as America's most popular book, glorified the American hero. The tales, in the words of the *New York Times*, "appeal not to a spirit of wild adventure so vividly portrayed in the dime novels, but to a kind of humdrum practical success that most boys saw clearly ahead of them." Thus Alger produced such serials as *Sink or Swim*, *Strive and Succeed,* and

Struggling Upward. In *Luck and Pluck* a robust lad leaves the farm with a few belongings tied to a handkerchief to seek fortune. He lives cleanly—and with luck and pluck—prospers so as to return in time to pay off the mortgage and save the homestead.

Radical changes in the nature of work and the composition of the workforce have ensued in the 20th century. In 1800 nine of 10 workers toiled on the farm. With the advent of technology and the industrial revolution the percentage decreased to two/thirds in 1850 and to 2.9 % in 1996. A spot on the assembly line took over from a place under the sun in the field. The revolution enabled the worker to produce in two hours what had taken twelve for the grandparent.

The average workweek fell off as follows:

1850	69.7 hours
1930	47.7 hours
1950	41.2 hours
1970	37.1 hours
1990	34.5 hours

Writing in 1972, Ahlstrom closed his 1,100-page volume on the history of religion in America with a few thoughts. In its early years the United States became "the land par excellence ... of a 'gospel' of work that was undergirded by the so-called Puritan Ethic." That ethic, which had long dominated the nation's religious heritage, was on the wane.

Change Occurs

"The notion of work as a spiritual calling fell out of sync with the mechanized work of mass production," wrote Perry Pascarella in the *New Achievers*. He traced, too, the invasion of women into the work force. In 1984 women constituted 44 per cent of employees. The author projected a 50/50 mix at the millennium. The percentage of families with no spouse at home during the day continues to rise.

An ethic based on production shifted to one of consumption. Pascarella claimed that work lost its social and spiritual implications narrowing the employee's rewards to economic benefits. Along the way people lost sight of the values of producing. Americans had been remembered for what they produced rather than consumed.

David J. Cherrington, the author of the *Work Ethic; Working Values and Values That Work*, referred to a poll concluding that younger workers are less work-oriented than middle-aged workers, and middle aged workers are less work-oriented than older workers. He observed a concurrent decrease in the number of articles devoted to the work ethic. The author declared the trends bear serious implications for motivating Americans.

The moral importance of work has diminished. A poll found that pride in craftsmanship ranked first as a motivator—as the most desirable outcome from work. Service to others came in fourth. Cherrington saw the results of the poll as representative of a shift from a work to a character ethic. Respondents deemed "feeling more worthwhile"—recognition and respect from others—as greater stimulants than the rendering of service.

Attention has turned to the leisure inherent in the seventh day God took off. A shorter workweek leads to the realization that life is something more than one's job. A theologian lamented the prevalence of death shortly after retirement, particularly by the best workers who had devoted themselves exclusively to their jobs. Sermons are now directed at workaholics—those with a compulsion to work incessantly.

A work force with a 50/50 balance between the sexes and young mothers leaving their children behind in the morning brings divisive pressures between the job and the family. Peter Senge entitled one chapter in the *Fifth Discipline* "Ending the War between Work and Family." In seminars Senge conducted, he ascertained that finding a balance between work and family to be the prime issue among those in attendance. Enlightened organizations, he avers, will confront the boundary between work and family, and integrate the personal interest of the worker with the aims of the company. A compact follows. The synergy between productive family life and productive work life militates against pressures that make success at work and success at home an "either/or" proposition. The conflict is not merely one of time but of values.

The Attributes of the Best Worker

Attitude. Pursuit of excellence. Persistence. Willingness to accept and bounce back from defeat. Those are the attributes great workers bring to their vocation.

Gehrig's coach in college at Columbia University noted that Gehrig was the most enthusiastic player he had ever led. That attitude affects all roles. In *Working*, Studs Terkel used a tape recorder to catch 134 men and women talking about what they do all day and how they feel about what they do. Dolores Dante says,

> I have to be a waitress. How else can I learn about people? How else does the world come to me? I can't go to everyone. So they have to come to me. Everyone wants to eat, everyone has hunger. And I serve them. If they've had a bad day, I nurse them, cajole them. Maybe with coffee I give them a little philosophy. They have cocktails, I give them political science.

Terkel visited a drugstore to interview Nimo, who notes that the work is important to him, but not to the world. Nimo's colleague intercedes. "You're very important. As far as this store is concerned you're more than important. (To others in earshot) People love him. He has a terrific following. They bring their babies in, they bring their grandchildren in to meet him." Another associate remarks that seventy percent of the people come in to see Nimo, who responds, "I don't know about that. Look around—at the people who do great things for humanity." The associates replies, "Oh, Nimo, you do something for humanity every day you stand there." Later the popular druggist reflected on a fellow employee, now dead, who refused remedies to an obviously stricken customer without a written prescription. Nimo adds, the customer would "walk around the block and come back to me. I'd say, 'I know you, you're solid. Oh sure, here's a pill. I would take a chance on humanity. I don't think that's a sin'."

Great workers strive to excel. A high school baseball coach recalled young Cal Ripken, now a legendary baseball player, as "totally dedicated to improving his skills. He would have a batting cage in his back yard and hit balls hundreds of times." Ripken described his philosophy of the game, "If I do it, I'll do it well."

John W. Gardner, Secretary of Health, Education and Welfare in the Johnson administration, was often quoted in an excerpt from his book *No Easy Victories*,

> An excellent plumber is infinitely more admirable than an incompetent philosopher. The society which scorns excellence in plumbing because plumbing is a humble activity and tolerates shoddiness in philosophy because it is an exalted activity will have neither good plumbing nor good philosophy. Neither its pipes nor its theories will hold water.

Persistence deserves applause. Edgar Guest wrote two twelve-line poems that were included in the section devoted to work in William Bennett's *Book of Virtues*. The opening lines in the poem entitled "True Nobility" state,

Who does his task from day to day
And meets whatever comes his way,
Believing God has willed it so,
Has found greatness here below.

Guest named this rhyme "Results and Roses."

The man who wants a garden fair,
Or small or very big
With flowers growing here and there,
Must bend his back and dig.
The things are mighty few on earth
That wishes can attain.
Whate'er we want of any worth
We've got to work to gain.
It matters not what goal you seek
Its secret here reposes:
You've got to dig from week to week
To get results or roses.

Mishaps take place. The setbacks that inevitably occur teach resilience and endurance. Ripken's father was fired as general manager of the Baltimore Orioles. Ripken commented, "Professionalism, the work ethic—I know it sounds trite but that's what my father taught us—that there's a certain way to do things, a way to go about it, and you do it, no more or less, regardless of the circumstances."

Ripken was the first recipient of the Most Valuable Player Award to have played on a losing team (sixth place). "I feel fortunate to know the losing side," he said. "Maybe you appreciate winning more. Maybe you're a better person for experiencing defeat as well as success. If you see only one side of it, you don't have the full picture."

Sports reporter Harvey Rosenfeld traced the Baltimore shortstop's career in a book entitled *Iron Man: the Cal Ripken, Jr. Story*. Ripken set records. He was one of two shortstops to win the Most Valuable Player Award twice. He established an American League record with 503 assists in a season and a record for both leagues for consecutive errorless games at his position. He established himself as the greatest home run hitter among shortstops ever to play. In 1991 he received the Roberto Clemente Award as the player who best exemplifies the game on and off the field.

A New York Yankee spokesman said, "Of all records, that was the most improbable to be broken. Certainly we expected the iron man record (of Gehrig) to be for all time." It wasn't. In 1996 Cal Ripken broke the mark.

Near the beginning of his career a 91-mile-per-hour fastball put a hole the size of a silver dollar in his helmet. He missed the next day, nursing the effects of the beaning. That marked the last day he was not in the Orioles' box score. Injury did not deter him thereafter, as he was hit on 42 occasions. One September he told his father he had sprained his left hand. His father, then the team manager, advised, "Put some tobacco juice on it and use the top hand. Let's go." The prescription worked. Ripken collected five hits and 13 total bases, an Oriole record. The succeeding manager said, "Cal has been fortunate to avoid injury, but he doesn't avoid injury. He's banged up like everybody else. He plays with pain, and he plays well with pain."

Ripken wants to play. The will is there. One blazing day the temperature soared toward 100 degrees and a coach came to take Ripken out. But Ripken insisted that he would not leave the field. On reaching his 1500th game he commented,

"The real reason I've played this long is not because I set out to do it; it's just I wanted to go and play, be in the line-up."

And he wants to excel. When asked how he could improve his fielding skill, he replied, "I want to know where I should be on every hitter." As a hitter he sought to know the strike zone better. Self-improvement has been an ongoing regimen. He said, "I take the game home with me, because you're always thinking how you can get better.... If I don't think about it, I'll make the same mistake again."

Rosenfeld, the author, tells of the relentless work ethic Ripken brings to the game. Early one season Cal was the first to arrive for what he thought was batting practice. Instead he served as the practice pitcher for his team mates. Rosenfeld noted, "It mattered little because he hit three home runs that day."

For Ripken, like Maslow, a hierarchy of values looms large. Ripken declared, "The best thing that can be said about an athlete, in my opinion, is that he is consistent and does his job time after time.... I can be a better glove, I can be a better kind of hitter.... in my short career, I've already met players who didn't seem to want it enough. Sure they could stay up here on their talent, but sometimes talent is not enough. It's your working habits. It's your desire, then it's your talent."

On Faith

God reigns

Faith is a centered act that involves the whole man. This ultimate concern is the central phenomenon in the person's life. Paul Tillich in the *Dynamics of Faith* writes, "Hardly a word in the religious language, both theological and popular, is subject to more misunderstandings, distortions, and questionable definitions than the word 'faith'."

Faith involves total surrender to the ultimate concern. Emotion is not the source, nor is faith subject to mere feeling. Tillich declared that faith is not a phenomenon among others in man's life. He stated, "If it is understood as what it centrally is, an ultimate concern, it cannot be undercut by modern science or any kind of philosophy."

God is the basic symbol, the source and object of unconditional love. To Him goes all honor. Saints are saints only because the source of all holiness is transparent through them.

Faith includes an element of skepticism not found in mystical experience. Doubt arises. Yes, there is a risk in confronting uncertainty. In fact, the risk in adopting one's ultimate concern is the greatest man can run, since if it proves to be a failure the meaning of life disintegrates.

A great debate centers on which comes first—being or consciousness. Tillich chooses the former. Faith accepts that which transcends ordinary experience. Faith is not an opinion, but a state.

The prime quality that triggers faith is courage. To Tillich, Luther marked the high point in the history of Christian thought. He fought for an immediate person-to-person relationship between man and God. Yet in Tillich's *The Courage to Be*, "The idea of God transcends both mysticism and the person-to-person encounter." Tillich closed his text by saying yes to the proposition, "The courage to be is rooted in the God who appears when God has disappeared in the anxiety of doubt."

Interned as a political prisoner in Russia, Mihailo Mihailov smuggled out some thoughts in 1974. He cited the fruits of obedience to an inner voice, the soul, not subject to rational control. To obey the inner voice; that is faith.

> Whoever follows his inner voice and saves his soul, learns empirically that, so long as the soul is not lost, the most important is not lost. From this knowledge comes the belief in the immortality of the soul. To obey the inner voice means nothing less than to define actions in terms of eternity.
>
> He who lets go of all outward trappings and decides from then on to obey his inner voice, which is only another name for faith, and then discovers to his amazement this mysterious yet real force at work not only inside himself but also in the outer world, realizes at the same time that he is not the master of this force and cannot use it just as he wishes. On the contrary, he begins to understand that everything in his life, indeed life itself, is entirely dependent on this mysterious inner power, which, in the language of religion, is called God.

Later Mihailov stated that inner striving is not voluntary, nor dependent on the desire or will of the person concerned. "All that depends on the person is whether he wishes to follow the inner impulse or not." Neither argument nor the will to believe can create faith. "Not my will, but thy will," said Jesus at Gethsemane.

The mysterious inner power called the soul baffles those searching for a human organ. A former monk discerns the soul as lying somewhere between understanding and consciousness. This ineffable element, neither corporeal nor mental, touches the imagination. Tending the soul is a sacred art.

For believers holding these views, faith emerges from God's grace.

Another Source: the Human Will

Others have chosen intellect over courage and subordinated courage to wisdom as the primary source of faith. In America William James, who called himself a pragmatist, delivered an address on the will to believe. In 1896, James spoke to the philosophical clubs of Yale and Brown, "I have brought with me tonight something like a justification by faith to read to you ... I mean an essay in justification of faith."

James asserted that his first act of free will shall be to believe in free will, which he further defined as "the sustaining of a thought because I choose to when I might have other thoughts." He compiled his remarks in his text *The Will To Believe*. In the preface he noted that religious fermentation always gives witness to the intellectual vigor of a society.

He contrasted man's faith and religion with the magnificent edifice of physical sciences with thousands of disinterested lives buried in its foundations. Intellectualism postulates that man's paramount duty is to escape error. In faith man must choose. James affirmed that truth exists, and man's mind is destined to attain it. Faith, an unalienable birthright of the mind, may grasp truth; it may not.

James spoke of man's nature that does not hinge on reason alone. He contended man not only lawfully may, but must, choose between propositions whenever a genuine option cannot by its nature be decided on intellectual grounds. He wrote, "For to say, under such circumstances, 'Do not decide, but leave the question open, is itself a 'passional' decision—just like deciding yes or no and is attended with the same risk of losing the truth."

The philosopher posited that there is truth, and the mind of man is destined to attain it. As an empiricist he noted that no concrete text of what is really true has ever been agreed upon. But mortals do not give up the quest for truth. Rather, they put their faith on its existence and roll up experiences that confirm it. The faith becomes true. James wrote, "Faith in a fact can help create a fact when each member in a social organism proceeds to his own duty with a presumption that others will do likewise."

The Famous Wager

The treatise alluded to Pascal's famous bet recorded in *Pensees*. Pascal outlined the following proposition: either God is, or he is not. To which view should man be inclined? Reason cannot decide the question. Thus the Frenchman's wager; "Let us weigh the gain and the loss involved in calling heads that God exists. Let us assess the two cases; if you win you win everything. If you lose you lose nothing." James called this celebrated page a last desperate "snatch at a weapon against the hardness of the unbelieving heart."

As a pragmatist James could write the *Varieties of Religious Experience* without having had such an experience himself. He did have a serious bout of melancholy that bore a religious aspect. A fear had become so invasive and powerful, he claimed, that "had I not clung to scripture—texts like 'the eternal God is my refuge; come unto me all ye that labor and are heavy-laden; I am the resurrection and the life'; etc. I think I should have grown really insane."

Thus faith from this view becomes a matter of will. To James,

> Religion, the adoption of moral beliefs, is a momentous option. If we believe the end is in our power, we will that the desired feeling, having, or doing shall be real, and real it presently becomes. 'Will you or won't you have it so?' is the most probing question we are ever asked; we are asked it every hour of the day, and about the largest as well as the smallest, the most theoretical as well as the most practical, things.

James concluded, "We stand on a mountain pass. Be strong and of good courage. Act for the best, hope for the best, and take what comes.... If death ends all, we can not meet death better."

The Initiative: God's or man's?

The debate on being versus consciousness extends into a practical realm. Does God take the initiative or does man realize on his own that God exists? Students of religious experience, unmediated union with God, recognize that direct communication between man and God has come about on the stimulus of both parties. Through grace God spoke to Saul on the road to Damascus. Others know God because He responded to an invitation.

Irrespective of the source of faith, the great peril lies in man's severance of communication through repression. A reviewer wrote of Kierkegard's *Sickness Unto Death* that the author "taught that most of us try all our lives to talk ourselves out of our moral and religious knowledge, because we do not want to be led to the sacrifices this knowledge commands."

Look at how they love one another. Faith can be seen in service. Tillich wrote, "Faith implies love; love lives in works.... Where there is ultimate concern there is the passionate desire to actualize the content of one's concern." Man is separated from others. He aspires, out of faith, for reunion. Thus faith is a matter of community, and Tillich pointed to the Jews, for, in their history, they document the ultimate and unconditional character of faith.

Faith Observed

Faith becomes palpable in a life—both that of the individual and that of the community. Rob Dowds, a youthful California resident, went to Indonesia in the fall of 1992. There he worked with a team belonging to Youth With a Mission. The band devoted three months to teaching and three months to application of the biblical message.

The foreigners were asked to preach. Natives gave great credence to itinerant speakers. One Sunday in Singaraja, the capital of the island of Bali, Dowds participated in a communion service. The local pastor requested that Dowds give a sermon to a congregation of 300 members.

Dowds reflected,

> I was exhausted from the heat and the mosquitos. I had not prepared a sermon. I had no outline. So I just preached on how we must rely on Jesus for healing. I talked about relationships. I observed that when we look at the cross we

recognize the importance of reconciliation. Nothing in my remarks pertained to physical healing.

At the end of his sermon he sat down. Later the pastor came up to him. In the native language, with which Dowds was unfamiliar, the pastor called for physical and spiritual healing for those in attendance. Dowds said,

> I thought the local clergyman had come to thank me. When I heard about the physical healing from an interpreter, I was put in a pickle. I didn't want to get involved. People started coming up. I struggled over what was happening. Then I prayed, "Okay, God, you know there's nothing I can do; you have to take over." I continued to pray. I didn't feel I had any responsibility for what was happening. Some people would cry. Others wailed.

A woman in her 80s came up to Dowds. He asked the interpreter what was wrong. He was told that the woman could not speak because of a problem with her larynx. I prayed, "Lord, do what you can." Then I asked her to speak. She could not. He prayed again for another five minutes. Slowly the woman began to articulate. Dowds noted, "It was a true miracle. The woman had not spoken in twelve years according to her son, a Muslim. I was astounded. I did not know what to believe."

The itinerant preacher along with the young men and women on his team aimed to deal with cultural matters. They wanted to establish credibility by addressing the needs of the community. But the word got out that the white people were performing miracles. The natives requested healing seminars. One Hindu group of 50 families in a village high on the hills feared a crop loss from a lack of rain. Dowds walked twelve miles to get there. He reported, "We all prayed for rain. That night it came—watering the crops and filling the river." That gave credibility to his work.

The twelve-member team split up. Others shared similar experiences. In all, there were 35 instances of healing. One student prayed for a blind man. The man said, "I feel as if someone was washing my eyes." On the following day the man could discern shapes. There were no physical signs of visual impairment, such as a cataract, that an ophthalmologist could detect.

The healing occurred in a country where the gospel is not welcome. Visitors had to be invited. Dowds said that the team exercised caution. He said, "The dramas to which we alluded could not be very pointed." The most radical instance involved a man with a foot deformed since birth. Four or five friends of Dowds prayed. Nothing happened at the outset. But further prayer caused the foot to be healed before the eyes of those on hand. "You could see it happen. It was completely unexplainable. I was blown away," Dowds said. The students bought the man a pair of tennis shoes.

Dowds has prepared a tract on physical healing. The essay declares that faith is required by both parties.

> First, you the person praying must allow the healing power to flow through you, just as it did with Jesus. Secondly, the person for whom you are praying needs to be able to conduct the healing power just like the woman in Luke 8:46-48.

After the bleeding woman brushed Jesus, He remarked, "Somebody touched Me, for I perceived power going out from Me" ... and two verses later to the recipient, "Your faith has made you well. Go in peace."

Another story of faith involves a lottery, a variation on Pascal's famous bet. Mary Jo Hancock never read Pascal, but, for her, God is more than a pensee. He is real. A mother of four she spoke one morning at a McDonalds restaurant. Mary Jo said, "I am an independent person. I tackle things over which I have control. I'm not a person to play the lottery; it's not part of my reality."

Mary Jo's early years had been chaotic. She had come from a dysfunctional family. Her mother had been an invalid, and her father had never accepted the mother's disability. Mary Jo said, "Every night he went into a tirade." Her mother suffered. Her father suffered also in thinking himself responsible and helpless. Mary Jo adopted survival skills. She took on the fanciful idea that she, a child, would take care of her parents. Later as an adult she unwittingly married a man with mental aberrations.

Yet she played the lottery when struck by an impulse or incentive, such as the occasion when a fellow at work told her he wanted to buy a lottery ticket for her in Maryland. "Pick your numbers," he said. She replied, "3-3-3" because she detected a pattern in her life that God's will manifested itself in the number 3. She had found that she picked the third car or apartment she looked at. Her associate counseled against her selection of the same three numbers, as she would have a better chance with different numbers.

She chose 369. The phone rang at the Holiday Inn. Room #369 needed service. She said to herself, "I'm going to win. My ship has come in." But again it did not. Yet she felt destined to win with some combination of threes.

Over a seven-year span she played the lottery twelve times without success. She wondered if destiny would favor her with the grand prize. She had always believed in numbers. The belief had helped her face the hurt and pain of childhood trauma; of later abuse and abandonment by her schizophrenic husband, leaving her with three children. She said, "It is necessary to believe there's a rainbow at the end. That's the essence of faith." The lottery motivated her to reach for a new life. "God promises; and I believed the whole way that he would keep his promises." But she never knew for sure whether abundance and the new life would come in the form she anticipated—the lottery.

She had chased the rainbow a long time. She knew she had no control over the lottery. She asked God, "Tell me which rainbow is real. God, I need to know, 'Are we going to win this lottery or not'?" She got a response, "All there is is love."

For six months she stumbled, wondering if the "Yes" were real. She could choose. From one view God is love; God is real. Or she could recognize, "I have my rainbow," as she recounted marriage to her second husband, the child of that union, and the three youngsters from her first marriage. She was content with both perspectives.

The lottery had served as a security blanket conveying the message that she had great value. Now she lives without the lottery as a comforter. She has her own focus, identity, and goal. She thanked God for providing the tool that allowed her to heal. In letting go of the lottery she could finish grieving over her invalid mother who was unable to be the mother Mary Jo had wanted. She said, "Mother told me that I had always been a special child with a special purpose. I know that through my fourth child unexpectedly born, as I had been, at age 41, I could experience the same kind of joy my mother had had with me."

Hancock summed up her story. She knows the power of God; of love. She gave up the lottery. She told her mother good-bye; her mother's work is done. She has her own work and a rainbow—a family that is whole. Love is acceptance by God. She concluded, "I accept that. I am aware that He has chosen me and I should quit denying His power. There is power in a woman loving her family. God will give me what I need."

Faith and Reason

In the grand scheme of life, whether yours or Mary Jo Hancock's, where does reason fit in? Are faith and reason compatible or are they at odds? Tolerance offers a compromise. The respective roles of these two forces—both deserving respect—have taken center stage since the Reformation.

Mythologist Joseph Campbell commented that the descent of the Occidental sciences from the heavens to the earth (from 17th century astronomy to 19th century biology), and their concentration today, at last, on man himself (in twentieth century anthropology and psychology), marks the path of a prodigious transfer of the focal point of human wonder.

As for the last of the disciplines named by Campbell, Tillich claimed it is "afraid of the concept of the soul, which seems to establish a reality that is unapproachable." He noted a few pages later in *The Dynamics of Faith* that neither scientific nor historical truth can affirm nor negate the truth of faith and vice versa.

In 1961 Ariel Durant joined her husband in completing the seventh volume in the *Story of Civilization*. The historians named the book the *Age of Reason* to cover the era in Europe from 1558 to 1648. In the preface they wrote, "The great debate between religion and science is the main current of the stream of modern thought." In the following volume they asserted, "The pervading theme is the great debate between faith and reason." Moving well into the 18th century in the ninth volume they reverted to the initial expression—"that pervasive and continuing conflict between religion and science."

Rather than take sides in debate, reason and faith could engage in an uneasy alliance. Thomas Jefferson wrote to his nephew in 1787, "Question with boldness even the existence of a God; because, if there be one, he must more approve of the homage of reason, than that of blindfolded fear.... Keep reason on the watch in reading books, including the New Testament."

All Christians hold that Jesus is Lord. For one denomination the essentials include two creeds and the Bible. Beyond that, that church relies on tradition and reason as guiding factors.

The force opposing faith is not reason but faithlessness, a sign of a torpid society. Dr. Abraham Kaplan presented a lecture entitled "Maturity in Religion." He said,

> Faith is not the evidence of things unseen; it is the substance of things hoped for. To my mind, the opposite of faith is not skepticism—skepticism is healthy and a mark of the mature mind. The opposite of faith is faithlessness. It is this which the religious life is setting itself against—the notion, not that there isn't anything to believe, but that there isn't anything worth believing in.

The American Creed

The 20th century saw two faiths at war. Whittaker Chambers wrote a book, *Witness*, with the preface directed as a letter to his children. As a former Communist, he told his children that communism was based on man's second oldest faith. That faith held power because it was based on a conviction by Karl Marx that "it is necessary to change the world." Adherents were willing to act on that conviction in a world that had lost that power. Chambers wrote:

> Communists are that part of mankind which has recovered the power to live or die—to bear witness for its faith. And it is a simple, rational faith that inspires men to live or die for it.... It is not new ... It is the great alternative faith of mankind. Like all great faiths, its force derives from a simple vision ... the vision of God and man's relationship to God.

> The communist vision is the vision of man without God.... It is the vision of man's displacing God as the creative intelligence of the world. It is the vision of man's liberated mind, by the sole force of its rational intelligence, redirecting man's destiny and reorganizing man's life and the world.

Communism did not prevail. The Berlin Wall came down. In March 1990 the newly elected president of Czechoslovakia, Vaclav Havel, addressed a joint body of the Congress and Senate. Rhetorically he asked, "How can the U.S. help us today? My reply is as paradoxical as the whole of my life has been. You can help us most of all if you help the Soviet Union on its irreversible but immensely complicated road to democracy." Democracy is a tenet the country holds dear. Havel concluded his remarks by quoting a founder of the United States, "When Thomas Jefferson wrote that 'governments are instituted among men, deriving their just powers from the consent of the governed,' it was a simple and important act of the human spirit."

Though Helen Keller was blind, she had a vision described in her book *Let Us Have Faith*. Like Havel, she attributed the country's unique heritage to the founders' belief in democracy. Author and retired state editor of the *Richmond Times-Dispatch* Thomas Howard reviewed this manuscript before publication. He suggested a paragraph or two on reading Thoreau's account of civil disobedience. He noted that in the United States impatient protestors can be dealt with legally until laws are changed. "That is the strength of a democracy," he wrote.

The pledge of allegiance contains the other essential elements in the American creed.

Faith provides the moral undergirding for right action. George Washington identified virtue or morality as a necessary spring of popular government. In his farewell address in

1796 he said, "Of all the dispositions and habits which lead to political prosperity, religion and morality are indispensable supports."

These indispensable supports move communities sharing the same convictions. In a lecture at Columbia University in 1958 Adolph Berle pointed to the contrast in the cultures of people in similar environments but different beliefs—in the lower Mediterranean region between Israel and its neighbors and, in America, Salt Lake City and Las Vegas. Berle contributed to a draft called the American affirmation in a report for the Rockefeller Brothers Fund:

> Faith, which modern students like to call a "value system," is the driving force in all societies. History, at all events, records no society without a value system; no strong society without a value system firmly held and followed; no enduring society whose values did not have a measure of universal validity.
>
> These value systems, past and present, have invariably centered on religion. Time may produce a society whose value system expresses itself in non-religious terms—a rationalist's religion, if you choose, and this has yet to occur ... by ironic paradox, Communist organization draws much of its strength from Christian doctrine, which it officially denies ... America, perhaps more than any other society, exemplifies this unfailing historical imperative. It was formed around a series of religious movements, giving dynamism to its evolving political organization. The Protestant Reformation stamp runs straight across the northern tier of the United States. Missionary Catholicism gave form and frame to the southwestern third of the American union. Wesleyan Baptist and Church of England power brought together the Central and Southern area, as Quakers gave substance and permanency to Pennsylvania. Later immigrant movements merely added to this emotional and spiritual heritage—the Mormons of Utah, Roman Catholics, Irish and Italian, in

the Northeast; Jewish tradition on the East coast and in the Midwest centers. To state an American outlook without recognizing this foundation would be a negation.

Deriving from and surrounding the core of religious faith, there is an ethical system.

The Major Religions in America

Christians, Jews, and Muslims are the three major religious groups in the United States.* The following sections attempt to capture the essence of each of the major faiths, which all center on God. The Christian section contains excerpts from and references to the New Testament and liturgy; the Jewish, the Old Testament; and Moslems, the Koran.

The Faith of Christians

JOHN 1:17

"For the law was given by Moses, but grace and truth came by Jesus Christ."

JOHN 3:16

"For God so loved the world, that he gave his only begotten Son, that whosoever believeth in him should not perish, but have everlasting life."

---

*Their population count nationally, according to the 1997 edition of the World Almanac, totaled 165, 4.3, and 5.1 million respectively. In the world the figures amounted to 1,928 (34%), 14 (.25%), and 1,100 (19%) million. Percentages for Americans can mislead, as some denominations (adherents of being) count infants, while others postpone baptism until children reach the age of 9 (when will and consciousness come into play).

John 15:5

"I am the vine, ye are the branches; He that abideth in me, and I in him, the same bringeth forth much fruit: for without me ye can do nothing."

The Baptismal Covenant

Celebrant	Do you believe in God the Father?
People	I believe in God, the Father almighty, creator of heaven and earth
Celebrant	Do you believe in Jesus Christ, the Son of God?
People	I believe in Jesus Christ, his only Son, our Lord. He was conceived by the power of the Holy Spirit and born of the Virgin Mary. He suffered under Pontius Pilate, was crucified, died, and was buried. He descended to the dead, On the third day he rose again. He ascended into heaven, and is seated at the right hand of the Father. He will come again to judge the living and the dead.
Celebrant	Do you believe in God the Holy Spirit?
People	I believe in the Holy Spirit, the holy catholic Church the communion of saints, the forgiveness of sins, the resurrection of the body, and the life everlasting.

The closing words in the creed hold that a mystical essence survives when the human heart stops beating. The soul endures forever.

FROM A PRAYER BOOK

Celebrant and People

Christ has died.
Christ is risen.
Christ will come again.

The Faith of Jews

Jews hold that an eternal God exists. God created the universe; He existed before the beginning; and He will exist after the end. Man lacks the capacity to perceive or understand the essence of God. God's qualities, if they do exist, are not to be known.

In man's futile attempt to define the nature of God, God becomes limited.

While Jews do not and can not define the essence of God, they do assert that men and women can know the nature of His attributes from His works. To Moses, in Exodus, God proclaimed himself the Lord, the Lord God, merciful, gracious, long suffering, and abundant in loving-kindness and truth, keeping mercy unto the thousandth generation, forgiving iniquity, transgression, and sin, and able to clear the guilty. Jews discern the attributes of mercy in this proclamation, and they can recognize his attributes in a personal relationship with Him.

In Genesis, at the outset of recorded human history, the writer announced that when God created man, He made him in the likeness of God. A man and a woman, then, should emulate His ways, for you and I are His spiritual and moral reflection. We can recognize the attributes inherent in God's acts. Your and my chief aim should be to make ourselves, as far as possible, similar to God—by making your and my acts similar to His. Thus may you and others construe your acts as holy; as sacred.

Simon the Just said, "The world is sustained by three things: by the Torah, by worship, and by loving deeds."

For Jews the first five books of the Old Testament, the Pentateuch, contain the spirit of God's law and will. In the Torah, biblical literature, and rabbinical interpretations of these books lie the meaning of Judaism. These sources state that the annals of the world are in the hands of man. God is not detached, nor oblivious—but a partner to men and women.

Evil is not inherent in a soul or society. Man is not born in a state of sin. Yet he does create suffering and behave cruelly towards his neighbor. The darker element in the human personality must be mastered. That is the struggle.

Man is essentially good, is capable of much good, and he must make human history move forward for human redemption. The purpose of the Jew, a salvational concept, is to be and act as a light to his and her people, history, and God.

Death is not the end. This world is a corridor in the world to come.

The Muslim Creed

God spoke directly to an illiterate Arabian for a 23-year span commencing in 610 A.D. Mohammed received a series of messages through the angel Gabriel that were recorded by Mohammed's companions in the Koran (Qur'an). God, communicating in the Arabic tongue, revealed himself in advocating worship of Allah, the one God. The holy book is designed to purify the soul from evil and prepare it for entry into heaven.

Allah alone is eternal. He is almighty, invisible, indivisible, just, loving, and forgiving. Belief in the one god is essential to a Muslim's faith.

The Koran contains the General Code of the Muslim world. Its authority is absolute in all aspects of religion, ethics, and science. Not a word has changed since its recording 13 centuries ago.

Mohammed, God's last messenger, interpreted and explained God's messages to those about him. The prophet's sayings compose the Hadith, a code of regulations for personal conduct. The sayings, known as Sunnah, are regarded as an encyclopedia of good manners and morals.

If the Koran and Hadith are silent on any question, Moslem jurists and scholars are consulted. Finally, private judgment is respected. Each individual can interpret scripture. Moreover, Allah hears man's prayers.

Worship of God through prayer, fasting, alms-giving, and a pilgrimage to Mecca constitute the four pillars of personal behavior. Abide by these commands to face the Day of Reckoning. On Judgment Day, nature's processes will cease and every Muslim will answer for his actions. The Koran depicts Heaven and Hell. Evil-doers will enter a blazing fire. "For them there is nothing but disgrace in this world and in the world to come an exceeding torment." Those who follow God will know joy in heaven. "To those who do good, there is good in this world and the home of the hereafter is even better."

The Faith of Americans

The American creed based in democracy is repeated daily in elementary schools— "one nation under God with liberty and justice for all."

On August 28, 1963 Martin Luther King, Jr., spoke at the Lincoln Memorial in the nation's capital:

> I have a dream today!
>
> I have a dream that one day every valley shall be exalted, every hill shall be made low, the rough places shall be made plain, and the crooked places shall be made straight and the glory of the Lord will be revealed and all flesh shall see it together...
>
> With this faith we will be able to work together, to pray together, to struggle together, to go to jail together, knowing that we will be free one day. This will be the day when all God's children will be able to sing with new meaning— "My country 'tis of thee; sweet land of liberty; of thee I sing; land where my fathers died, land of the pilgrim's pride; from every mountain side, let freedom ring." ...
>
> Let freedom ring from every hill and molehill of Mississippi, from every mountainside, let freedom ring. And when we allow freedom to ring, when we let it ring from every village and hamlet, from every city and state, we will be able to speed up that day when all of God's children—black men and white men, Jews and Gentiles, Catholics and Protestants—will be able to join hands and to sing in the words of the old Negro spiritual, "Free at last! Free at last! Thank God Almighty, we are free at last."

Amen.

On Family

"It is not good that the man should be alone; I will make him an help meet for him," said the Lord God in Genesis. A few verses later Old Testament readers read, "Therefore shall a man leave his father and his mother and shall cleave unto his wife, and they shall be one flesh." And in the sacrament of matrimony listeners hear Genesis paraphrased, "What God has joined together, let no man rend asunder."

James Dobson's book, *Dare to Discipline*, passed the 2,000,000 copy mark in 1992. Dobson proclaims that the principles of good parenting are eternal. The inspired concepts in scripture are just as valid for the 21st century as they were for ancestors. Men and women should heed the lessons reflected in the accumulated experience of 20 billion parents across more than 5,000 years. The jacket of Dobson's book acknowledges that a Judeo-Christian system of values permeates this work.

A doctor from the Harvard Medical School recorded his thoughts on the same theme. Dr. Armand M. Nicholi, Jr., observed that there was more wisdom in the Bible than in all the scientific knowledge acquired by man since time began. He wrote,

> What strikes me as I read and reread these documents is that the Creator is singularly unimpressed by what most of us give highest priority to—our achievements, our success, our education, our wealth, our listing in Who's Who or the

Social Register, the amount of economic or political or intellectual influence we wield. The Great Commandment makes clear that our lives must focus first and foremost on our relationships. First our relationship with the Creator, and, secondly, our relationship with others.

Genesis points to the family as man's oldest social institution, and the truth in the commandments is vindicated by the species' experience in billions of instances spanning thousands of years. What is that truth? In an essay Chester E. Finn, Jr., formerly an assistant secretary in the U.S. Department of Education, replied, "Two parent families are good for children, one parent families are bad, zero parent families are horrible." The acceptance of this proposition, he added, is a "whole lot more important than stopping smoking, lowering cholesterol levels, or recycling aluminum cans."

The family arose, too, to create children, care for infants, and educate and socialize the young. Dobson asserts that the parents' relationship with the child is modeled after God's relationship with man. The youngster observes and learns from his parents about God's two predominant natures—His unfathomable love and His justice.

But have we forgotten God and disregarded His Holy Ordinances, Dobson asks? So it appears. Near the end of his book, *How We Live,* Victor R. Fuchs noted, "One of the most persistent themes that emerges from the data in this book is the fading role of the conjugal family as the major institution in the United States society."

The Impact of the 1960s

Down with institutions! That cry became the mantra of the late 1960s. The federal government sent young men and women to Vietnam. Large numbers of men evaded the draft, going to Canada or, for conscientious objectors, to prison. The aphorism, "My country, right or wrong," grew obsolete.

At home some of the best and the brightest rebelled. No longer would reason prevail in the pursuit of the truth. When rational statements failed to still a student uprising, the president of Harvard, the nation's oldest educational institution, called in police to restore order. Churches were ignored for preaching the sanctity of matrimony in an era of free love.

For children this was the Age of Aquarius. Don't trust anyone over 30. Youngsters insisted on letting their hair grow to their navels to ally peers against parents.

Decades later Christopher Buckley wrote an essay entitled, "What did you do in the war, Daddy?" He cited Dr. Arthur Egendorf, a Vietnam veteran and the principal author of the *Legacies of Vietnam*. Those who did not go, suffer from a vague malaise, claimed Egendorf, a clinical psychologist.

> If there is a major strand that is played out among the nonveterans, it's this whole thing about nonengagement, noncommitment. Service got a bad name in the last war. People who didn't serve felt vindicated for keeping clean. And the main cost of all that is much more social than in any obvious sense individual. You see a declining trust in public institutions of all sorts.

Forget a sacred rite pledging "until death do us part."

The self became sovereign. "Do your own thing" became a cliché. Self-fulfillment replaced self-sacrifice, a commitment to others, and an institutional obligation as recounted by David Popenoe in *Life Without Father* and Barbara Dafoe Whitehead in the *Divorce Culture*. Marriage became less an institution expressing society's goals and more a personal, voluntary relationship to make or break at will in the pursuit of happiness. Personal growth superseded duty, service, and sacrifice.

Rob Corcoran of Richmond, Virginia, who has devoted his life's work to Moral Rearmament, talked bemusedly about the American dream in his home. He said,

> We expect the absence of pain. Yet difficulties are a part of life. They can't be avoided. Family disintegration arises from the unwillingness to work through our difficulties. We think about how we can achieve our goals and our expectations as opposed to our partner's. Last Saturday I saw the parents of kids at the soccer field. The mother and father had parted without apparent cause. People leave their mates out of boredom.

Women's liberation promised the happy life. No longer would wives be subjugated by patriarchal inventions—marriage and the conventional nuclear family. The National Organization of Women held in its founding statement "that a true partnership between the sexes demands a different concept of marriage, an equitable sharing of the responsibilities of home and children and of the economic burdens of their support." This concept, calling for an equal division of domestic and public labor, faced the knowledge that no human society existed where males provided as much child care as females. Inevitably tensions over the change in roles arose.

The tension extended to the job, too. Should the young mother attend to her infant or the work itself? Nicholi's clinical experience indicated clearly, "that no mother with young children can do both at the same time without sacrificing one or the other, the quality of the work, or the quality of child care."

Equal pay on the job enabled the wife to free herself from a boring husband. A clergyman lamented that women entered their marital vows with a parachute. A *New Yorker* cartoon portrayed a suitor on bended knee getting an affirmative nod with the reply, "OK, but what's our exit strategy?" Fuchs, an economist, saw the trend in divorce as self-confirming. The increase in the probability of a break-up contributed to the rise in the number of women at work. Wives and mothers would not be put in economic peril if their marriage dissolved. Nobel Prize winner Gary S. Becker on an analysis of the economics of marriage concluded, "Couples divorce when they no longer believe they are better off by staying married. In particular, divorce rates grow when women's earnings are higher compared with those of men."

Divorce Becomes Popular

Thus the opening sentence of Barbara Whitehead's book states, "Divorce is now part of everyday American life." Popenoe wondered if the lifestyle of a single parent gains social acceptance as this tolerant attitude accords with the contemporary celebration of diversity. That notion caused him to write a book to convince readers that "if we continue down the path of fatherlessness, we are headed for social disaster."

Standards are lowered. In a recent poll citizens were asked their views on children born out of wedlock. Seventy per cent of the respondents between 18 and 34 years of age replied there should be no moral reproach; for those over 55, the response was 29 percent. Should a couple stay together for the children? In 1962, 51 percent said, "Yes."; in 1985, 18 percent. Public anxiety dissipated, and thus concern as a social problem diminished. Divorce was erased as a category to measure social deviancy.

The sacrament of marriage, attendant with a "for richer for poorer" promise, became a contract dependent on whim. No-fault divorce legislation shifted the leverage from the spouse who wished to preserve the union to the departing party. California, Arizona and Utah enacted laws to make divorce simple and trouble-free. Those states licensed electric divorce machines dubbed "quick-court" for placement in public buildings.

The federal government adopted policies to divide the family. Entitlement programs funneled monies into homes with children where the father was absent. Better that he stay away, for if he returned as a married husband, the subsidies ceased.

Fuchs declared that the expansion of government at the expense of the family is exacerbated when public assistance is tendered only if individuals exploit outside sources for subsidies. Nursing homes, involving institutional care, qualify for reimbursement while home care does not. Fuchs wrote, "Public policy influences how we die as well as how we live."

The primacy of self, the force of woman's liberation, a change in culture, and the impact of governmental policy precipitated trends that provoked Popenoe to remark, "At no time in history with the possible exception of Imperial Rome has the institution of marriage been more problematic than it is today."

The Impact on Children

Today the chance of the first marriage ending in divorce is close to 50 percent. Divorce, once rare, now affects 45 percent of the children, who, Whitehead asserted, have been "disenfranchised." She concluded that the damage the young people suffer poses a radical redistribution of hardship, so divorce can not be viewed as a morally neutral act.

The fault line in the late 1960s is evident in a host of trends. The United States has the highest teen pregnancy rate in the world. Surveys show that in 1950, 27 percent of America's girls at age 18 had experienced sexual intercourse; by 1988 the percentage had increased to 56 percent. Inevitably the count of infants born out of wedlock rose—from one in 13 in 1965 to one in three in 1995. Those youngsters lack two parents at home.

Under the stimulus of federal funding, the Virginia governor's office conducted a series of meetings in 1997 to lower out-of-wedlock births. The Department of Health prepared materials for the Secretaries of Public Safety, Education, and Health and Human Resources. Popenoe claimed juvenile delinquency looms largest on the public mind. In talking points for the secretary of public safety, a draft noted 72 percent of the nation's adolescent murderers and 60 percent of America's rapists grew up in homes without fathers. Seventy percent of the juveniles in state reform institutions were raised in single or no parent situations.

The Secretary of Education was advised that such youngsters were more likely to drop out, score lower on standardized achievement tests, and get inferior grades. The secretary of health document reflected a higher rate of suicide and the given that antisocial behavior is passed along to the next generation. The risk of becoming a teenage mother is 11 percent for children raised by both parents but 27 percent for children raised by single mothers.

The Virginia governor's office identified Dr. Kathy Wibberly as the expert in preparing the materials. Wibberly averred that children without two parents face an array of odds against them. She said, "You can tell kids with a mother and father at home by their social skills, impulse control, grades, and values." She added that wholesome values are not transmitted to the next generation by single mothers, as they don't point out that they erred.

Statistics fail to reveal the emotional and psychic toll on children with divorced parents. In a California study the initial reaction of over 90 percent of the children was an "acute sense of shock, intense fears, and grieving which the children found overwhelming." After five years, more than a third were moderately to severely depressed.

Dr. Nicholi found the same negative consequences in a study of several hundred drop-outs from Harvard for psychiatric reasons. They shared two characteristics—a marked isolation and alienation from their parents and an overwhelming apathy and lack of motivation. That the malaise occurred at Harvard rebuts those who attribute the social damage to poverty. In fact, Fuchs reports that 9 % of Harvard's class of 1985 consisted of Asian-Americans who tended to come from low-income families in which English had been a second language. Their educational achievement was attributed to the importance of scholarship in Asian societies and a strong family structure to transmit this value.

"You can't try to explain the data as a poverty issue," exclaimed Dr. Wibberly—of Asian descent herself. A hand-out she distributed said that a 1988 study found that the proportion of single parent households in a community predicts its rate of violent crime and burglary, but the community's poverty level does not. A 1993 report on underclass behavior reported,

> Young black men raised in single parent families on welfare and living in public housing are twice as likely to engage in criminal activities compared to young black men raised in two parent families also on welfare and living in public housing.

The circumstances demand that Americans treat these matters similar to a policy the nation would adopt to face a major menace. Finn closed his essay by asserting,

> If we have any serious expectation of winning this new war on behavioral poverty, we're going to need not only the

imagination to devise strategies suited to victory but also the resolve to see them through.

Government programs have proliferated to redistribute income. Fuchs claimed such measures have harmed the family, and he noted the damage is increased when public assistance is extended only if individuals use non-family sources for subsidized services. Recognize, he exhorted, the potential conflict between the family and expansion of redistributive government.

Measures to Counter Trends

One measure enacted at the national level, known as the Personal Responsibility and Work Opportunity Reconciliation Act, provided financial incentives through grants to states to set higher moral standards. Rather than enact a quick divorce court statute, Louisiana passed legislation in 1997 favoring a "high-test" union through a covenant-marriage law. This contract, optional to future husband and wife, extended the waiting period from six to 24 months for eligibility for a no-fault divorce.

The contract calls for counseling before marriage or divorce. Corcoran, a father of three and Moral Rearmament worker, argues that counselors should favor marriage and try to keep couples together. He opposes a "trial separation." Save the marriage not the individual. The role of counselors, according to Whitehead's *Divorce Culture*, arose from the popular secular thinking that suggested experts should take over from religious leaders.

Better yet, religious leaders, seeing matrimony as a sacrament rather than a contract with legal implications, should reclaim their ground.

Men and women can benefit from millennia of experience

that reveal that marriages are more likely to fail the younger the participants, and the more acquainted the twosome are at the outset, the more likely the union will endure. A serious issue, tantamount to a national defense policy, calls too for an injection of humor. A guest entering Groucho Marx' home asked, "How's your wife?" "Compared to what," the host rejoined. On departure the invitee said, "I'd like to say good-bye to your wife." Marx responded, "Who wouldn't?" On a similar refrain a veteran of 51 years in a marriage attributed its length to his wife's "always being right." "If a man speaks in the forest, and there is no wife to hear him, is he still wrong?" asked one wag.

The dons cited here regard the nuclear family as a signal achievement. But times have changed. Since women now leave home for work, husbands must assume a new role and view parenting as a cooperative activity. Both parents are to engage in the day-to-day care of their children from birth onwards. Popenoe wrote that the new father is expected to be more engaged with children and involved with housework.

Others look to the village school to fill the gap. But Finn, a veteran of the U.S. Department of Education, pointed out that an 18-year-old with a perfect attendance record has spent only 9 percent of his life under a school roof. Meanwhile at home but 16 percent of all households now "fit the traditional concept of mother, father, and two children, with dad the bread-winner." On viewing these conditions in America, Whitehead commented, "The matter of addressing the question of what we are doing (the village) evades the question, 'What are individual parents obliged to do for the sake of children?'"

Fuchs traced the traditional concept to the Industrial Revolution when the conjugal family became the means to provide physical and psychological support for many years after birth. The family alone was charged as the social institution to "transform a biological organism into a human being." Later he remarked about the unusual pace of change regarding divorce, household living arrangements, and the labor force participation of married women with small children.

One of the greatest achievements of the modern nuclear family lies in the extended nurturing of children by their biological parents. The children benefited most.

The stakeholders, the children, have become disenfranchised. They suffer the damage. Whitehead contrasted loss as the dominant theme in literature for children with liberation in adult literature in the post nuclear family era.

The Importance of the Mother to the Baby

Some years in a human life are more important than others. A Newsweek article reported, "Ninety percent of human brain growth occurs during the first three years, and it is aided immensely by being held often as a baby, by a loving adult who sings, talks and reads to a child."

For the first 12 to 18 months the mother has the primary role because of the enormous physical and psychological benefits from breast feeding. Commentators James Q. Wilson and Richard J. Herrnstein, in their book *Crime and Human Nature*, described the bond between mother and child during this span as critical. Lacking such an attachment criminal behavior is more likely. They reported that chronic recidivists begin their misdeeds at an early age, and they concluded this behavior points to "constitutional" and "familial" factors.

Best seller Dobson characterized the toddler as a hard-nosed opponent of law and order. The father helps the mother discipline the rebellious tot, and a survey of 26,000 children followed from birth to age four reported somewhat higher IQ scores if the father were present.

Distinctions between Mother and Father

Vive la différence! Men and women differ. Popenoe listed distinctions in aggression, cognitive skills, sensory sensitivity, and sexual and reproductive behavior. In the matter of sex a man is both dad and cad. Cultural sanctions arose to favor the former tendency. Popenoe claimed marriage was instituted in all societies to prevent men, more promiscuous and polygamous by nature, from straying sexually. The sacrament of matrimony keeps men attached to their mates so that the children will have the best chance to survive and thrive.

J. Q. Wilson, a criminologist at the University of California, paraphrased this tendency more colorfully in his opening remarks on gender; "Nature has played a cruel trick on humankind. It has made males essential for reproduction but next to useless for nurturance." In short, men are not as biologically attuned to being committed fathers (dads) as women are to being committed mothers.

Fathers teach their children self-control, which is particularly critical for sons, as males are more aggressive. Through play and competitive games children learn to express their innate aggressiveness positively. Fathers set limits. Youngsters learn about justice and fairness from their dads. Dobson observes that children typically identify their parents, especially their fathers, with God.

While sons and daughters discern God in their parents, the fathers as male role models are the first and most important men to girls. Constructive heterosexual relationships arise from the trust and intimacy between Dad and his daughter.

All children learn about male-female relationships by seeing how their parents relate to one another.

Not only do males and females differ by nature, but they differ in style as parents. The difference is important for healthy child development. The father supplies wings. He teaches independence, risk-taking, and challenge. His efforts push the growing child toward autonomy.

Mother furnishes roots. She exemplifies and preaches care for others. She shows sympathy. From mom the child gains a sense of security.

A Model Family

Melvin Law, the black Chairman of the Richmond Public School Board, addressed the Richmond First Club in 1997. He recounted his own upbringing with an illiterate father and a mother with but four years in school. Law told club members about the virtue of the two-parent, single-wage-earner family. Children are worth the sacrifice of a stay-at-home mother until children reach the first or second grade. He bemoaned the large number of complaints on school closings after four inch snowfalls, as the parents looked to the schools for child care.

In his own home Law pointed to his wife Dolly. He cited among the greatest of his blessings Dolly's staying at home to raise four children, "forgoing the opportunity to keep up with the Joneses." She volunteered to assist at her children's schools and occasionally served as a substitute teacher. Law remembered an instance when Dolly was absent when their daughter, Debbie, arrived home. Debbie asked, "Where were you? You weren't here." They recalled their daughter's anxiety at the time.

Law passes on the plaudits to his wife in talking about the

success their children, now grown, have experienced. The oldest son, Melvin Jr. works as an orthopedic surgeon. Dolly said, "We were told at his graduation from the Harvard Medical School that Melvin Jr. was one of six black spine surgeons in the country." The doctor is married to a housemom with two children.

Their second son, Mark, also received a doctorate to become a cornea specialist. Daughter Debra Michelle, after gaining a masters degree in health administration, devotes herself to that occupation at the Medical College of Virginia. The youngest son, a graduate of the University of Virginia, toils as an investment counselor with the VanGuard Corporation in Pennsylvania, where he takes graduate courses in business at Penn State.

The Essentials

How does a family grow to become so healthy? Richard and Linda Eyre of McLean, Virginia, raised nine children and wrote a book about their experience after consulting with the 50,000 parents in HomeBase, which they lead. They identified certain elements—rules, allocation of resources, and traditions—as keys to success.

"Children look for limits and the security they give," wrote the Eyres. A 16 year old in the family noted, "Rules give us freedom." In the Eyres' household the parents are in charge. They establish laws and administer discipline. With that responsibility they discuss the rules with their progeny at the dinner table, asking, "What are the laws that would make our family safer, happier?"

Discipline and Rules

A child replied, "In every single meeting we have my parents tell us … that if we didn't love you we wouldn't have laws and wouldn't care what you did and we would just let you do whatever you want."

The purpose of the laws drafted by the Eyres under the scrutiny of their children is to teach, not to control. Consequences follow when rules are disobeyed. The father and mother forgive whenever the children ask, and the adults apologize as they make mistakes.

Dobson, referring to lessons expounded two millennia ago, quoted Ephesians, "Children, obey your parents in the Lord, for this is right." If the mother is challenged defiantly, she must act decisively. Dobson agreed with the proverb permitting occasional use of the rod. Spanking, if undertaken, should be applied infrequently to a child from 18 months to 10 years.

The adoption of a permissive attitude when confronted by a defiant child leads to disaster. Dobson defined such as an "absence of effective parental authority." He wrote, "A boy or girl who knows love abounds at home will not resent a well-deserved spanking. One who is unloved or ignored will hate any form of discipline."

The effects from the framing and application of rules become manifest as the youngsters reach maturity. Through reward and punishment children develop self-control and responsible behavior. Dobson wrote, "When a child asks, 'Who's in charge?' Tell him."

Positive Signs of Affection

When the child mutters, "'Who loves me?' take him in your arms and surround him with affection." Dobson observed that for decades pediatricians have known that an infant who is not loved, touched, or caressed will often die of a condition called marasmus. Yet there was a time when hugging was verboten. Dobson claimed the lessons of history were overturned in the 1920s when wisdom on how to rear children shifted to experts.

As an infant Ann Leake of Hopewell, Virginia was exposed to the thinking of one such household authority, the pediatrician Luther Holt, who opposed picking up a baby when it cried or spoiling the child with too much handling. "My mother loved me, but I was fed by the clock, not by my cries. I did not receive nurturing hugs. As I grew up I felt insecure." The theory that caressing a child would spoil it proved wanting.

Mrs. Leake studied at and graduated from the Duke University School of Nursing. There she became exposed to the value of touching as taught by Ashley Montagu. She learned that "mothering" reduced the mortality rate for infants under one year. The physiological benefit stemmed from the stimulus of touch to the nervous system, which triggers the release of hormones like insulin. Holding infants lowers the level of a stress hormone, which, at high levels, kills important immune cells.

"In my next life, I want Ann to be my mother," a woman told Ann's husband Preston on a tour of England. Ann Leake has typed a hand-out headlined, "Hugging is healthy." This miracle drug improves blood circulation as doctors discern the increase of hemoglobin, which supplies oxygen to the heart and brain. The need for a hug endures through life. Indeed "Regular hugging can actually prolong life," Ann Leake recorded in her notes.

The benefits are psychological too. Infants feel secure when they are picked up as they cry. Mrs. Leake spoke about the development of a sense of trust. She recalled an instance in which she caught her grandchild cheating in a game. She said, "I held the child and told her, 'I love you, but I don't like what you did.' My granddaughter gave me a 'I can't believe you' look (astonished that she could still be loved) and said, 'I won't do that again'."

On a Valentine's Day, Abby, in her column, urged husbands to say those three little words to their wives. (A jocular male wrote, "I'll cook tonight.") Words matter. The fourth principle of HomeBase holds, "It is better to give positive attention to good behavior—than to give negative attention to bad behavior." The Eyres elaborated with the statement that parents need to give more praise and less criticism.

The Reverend Thom Blair, the rector of St. Stephens Church in Richmond, Virginia, talked from the pulpit about David, his good friend and fellow minister in St. Louis. David's father had been undemonstrative, never showing his feelings. David drew from his father's reticence that he could not please his father, for his Dad's "love was not there." The father died in David's early 30s. When they cleaned up the father's bedroom David found a box under the bed. In the box were the clippings of a lifetime of David's accomplishments—the records in the school paper, the ribbons the son had won, and the citations on the honor roll. Blair commented, "What a revelation and a shock. The father had stronger feelings but he had managed to hide them. For David it was literally redemptive, but a lot of damage had been done."

So tell members of the family that you love them. Verbal affirmations outweigh material gifts. "Talk to your kids, leave them notes," as communication is the single most important aspect of teaching family values, according to a Massachusetts Mutual Life Insurance Company tract.

The life insurance company pamphlet outlines several measures for parents to show their affection by devoting hours and days to their children. Fathers and mothers are exhorted to take their children to their jobs occasionally so that kids can learn about the workplace and their parents' role there. The entire family can share experiences at mealtimes and hold family meetings to confront specific issues as they arise.

Nicholi responded vehemently to a popular bromide. He wrote, "We use the cliche—'It's the quality and not the quantity time that counts.' But time and emotional accessibility are like the oxygen we breathe. Although the quality of the oxygen is important, the quantity determines whether we live or die."

A *New York Times* article reported that the average youngster on high school graduation had devoted 30 per cent more time to watching television than attending school. The typical child aged two to five spent 30 hours weekly and just 5 hours less in the following six years in front of the TV set. The set serves as a babysitter in many homes, a situation, to Nicholi's mind, that results from and causes parental inaccessibility. (Another pundit suggests turning off the car radio for family conversation.)

The effects of attention to this babysitter are not comforting. A surgeon general's report held that television viewing reduces, rather than aids, children's interests in reading and books. The greater the number of hours in front of the television set the lower the achievement test scores. Further, the television curriculum molds the character of youth.

Former U.S. Secretary of Education William Bennett compiled the *Book of Virtues* to promote moral literacy. Parents can pass on those virtues. Retired *New York Times* reporters, Fred and Grace Hechinger, wrote, "Future readers are created by mothers and fathers who read to their children from infancy, read to them during quiet moments of the day and read them to sleep at night."

But what if the father is illiterate? Melvin Law, Chairman of the Richmond School Board, reflected on his upbringing. He recalled, "My father spent but seven days in school. He left school on the day my grandfather died. My mother left school after the fourth grade, but they both knew education provided the means to overcome poverty and ignorance."

No welfare system existed in 1899 to help a family survive economically. Law's father, the oldest of four boys, was farmed out to work for a white family out of state from his seventh through 14th year. He went home once a year. The deprivation heightened his sense of family that he carried with him to death.

Yet, Law claims,

> My dad taught me more about literacy than anyone, although he could not read or write. In 1943 a retired school teacher visited our house to sell Compton Encyclopedias. My mother "humphed" at the $85 cost. My father asked, "Will they help the children?" The teacher replied positively, "If you see to it that the kids read the books, which will link them with other parts of the world."

The father promised to do his part, and Law's parents bought the set on an installment plan. Law was unaware then that his father could not read. Daily the father asked, "Have you read the book? Tell me something about your reading." Law said, "That was his way of testing. I would tell him about animals, birds, the Euphrates River."

In the second year of the daily conversations Law and his sister found a sales slip in a Compton edition with an "X" mark opposite his father's name. In asking their mother about it they learned about his illiteracy. Law remembered, "My sister and I then taught my father how to sign his name. He was really proud when he signed a paper." Law's father took his son to Charlestown, West Virginia as an eighth grader when the boy was a Golden Horseshoe winner for academic achievement. Law said, "My father's persistence on a daily basis showed to me the importance of reading. His $85 investment paid off."

Relevance of Family Traditions

The Eyres, parents of nine youngsters, listed traditions based on shared values as a critical element in life's most important opportunity and difficult challenge—that of building a family and raising children. Rituals hold the family together. They number good-bye kisses, bedtime stories, and dinners together as daily reminders that the members are connected. The parents assert those occasions provide the next generation the opportunity to talk about the boys' and girls' experiences outside family life and furnish the capital to face stress or conflict.

Each young Eyre has a memory book to record, if she or he wishes, rides down the Snake River, games at supper, feeding the homeless, or cutting a Christmas tree. Daughter Sarah, writing from Bulgaria at 23, elicited memories of Christmas stockings and Santa. "I miss simple things," she noted and recalled her affection for her brothers and sisters. In the book's postlude one child wrote, "The memories I have from our family traditions ... I wouldn't trade for anything." and another, "I feel so thankful for our little on-the-spot dinner talks."

Mother and father express love to their children through hugs, words, and attentiveness.

The Extended Family Ahead of the Village

Between the village and parents with children lies the extended family. Melvin Law traces his parents' enthusiasm for education to aunts who were teachers. Relatives provide support, love, and wisdom. Dobson spoke to the practices prior to the intervention of experts. When the first baby arrived a century ago aunts, sisters, and grandmothers assisted in teaching the new mother how to care for her infant.

In his preface Fuchs thanked, in addition to his loving parents and a brother, the uncles, grandparents, and in-laws for their affection and guidance. That affection comforts the family in sad moments as well. An *Atlantic Monthly* article described the solace offered by a mother's twelve siblings and her husband's three brothers when a daughter was murdered.

Ann Leake's husband, Preston, has pursued the genealogy of his family since retirement as a chemist. Leake entered 12,000 names in his computer and published an edition tracing 1,448 descendants through ten generations of one branch starting in the village of East Leake in England. He spoke of the fruits of his research. An 84-year-old cousin proofread the material. A nephew whose parents were divorced spoke to Preston at his brother's funeral. The genealogy prompted him to say, "I'm proud to be a Leake." Preston sees the history as producing a connectedness with "fellow man."

The end notes in Leake's publication conclude with a quote from an article entitled Ties that Bind:

> Genealogy is rewarding because it yields immediate results no matter at what level you choose to become involved, from the filling out of a simple family pedigree chart to the writing of a family history. It is guaranteed to draw you closer to your relatives, give you a greater appreciation for the history of America and the part your ancestors played in it,

> and provide you with a sense of belonging in this often hectic and rootless society in which we live....
>
> Genealogy also teaches that while wars, customs, and even governments change, some things are eternal — love, pride in children, devotion to country, sadness at the death of a loved one, and joy at the success of a crop or a new job. Through genealogy, we are connected very powerfully to the past, and also to the future.

Parents foster three senses in their children.

Cultivating the Moral Sense

The first is a moral sense. Wilson wrote that at an early age children can tell by intuition the difference between good and bad. A young person can recognize that breaking a promise, stealing flowers, and kicking a harmless animal are immoral. Parents affirm the intuitive knowledge through schooling in moral instruction. The Laws taught honesty, compassion, and truthfulness to their children.

Law referred to his father who, though illiterate, quoted time and again a favorite passage in Hebrews; "Follow peace with all men, and holiness, without which no man shall see the Lord." Law and his wife attempted to set civil standards. Alcohol, tobacco, and profanity were not allowed in their home. Law said, "We told the kids not to laugh at people for their misfortune. We forbid the word "ugly' as its use hurts."

Wilson noticed the results from moral instruction. The positive relationship between the parental ties and sociable behavior is universal. Secure children are confident and easy to be with. He wrote,

> We learn to cope with the people of the world because we learn to cope with members of the family. Those who flee the family flee the world bereft of the former's affection,

tutelage, and challenges. They are unprepared for the latter's tests, judgments, and demands.

Dr. Nicholi identified a spiritual dimension as a common denominator in a strong, healthy family. The Corcorans, whose parents, like themselves, devoted their lives to Moral Rearmament, send their children to public schools within Richmond's corporate limits. Corcoran said, "Our family is not just for ourselves but for others, and others are welcome into it. We welcome differences rather than fear them." He noticed neighbors home-schooling their children, because the parents wanted to protect their offspring from the evils of the world—crime, media, and drugs. He added, "They become cocoons and isolated. There's tremendous fear of what's out there. We have a role to contribute to the community. It's not just what the kids can get out of school but what they can put in."

Corcoran spoke about faith. Children learn better by observation than talk, but his family has discussed behavior in the context of situations. His son Neil, as a seventh-grader, had gone to his middle school on a day when potentially polarizing, racist graffiti appeared on the building. Corcoran said, "Neil told us that he had prayed in his home room that no one would get hurt. We had not suggested prayer. A black classmate, with whom he was not close, went over to Neil to offer to accompany him as they shifted rooms." Neil's father observed an inner sense, a quiet central part of his son's life. He recalled another instance when Neil said, "God yanked me along in the right direction."

The Second Sense: Financial

The second sense with which parents endow their children is financial—the stewardship of dollars and cents. Mother and father offer guidance on money, the element the Eyres defined as the allocation of resources.

For their children the Eyres outlined a program designed to develop self-reliance, gain the discipline of delayed gratification, and offer opportunities to make good decisions. The youngsters learned to earn through payment for household duties, which were distributed fairly.

Earnings for the youngest were registered in a family check book. The kids recorded and kept track of the amount. Each child computed the interest on his or her deposits. A 10% share was reserved for savings. As they grew older, the Eyre children wrote checks on the account to purchase clothing. They were free to make mistakes.

On reaching fourteen, the young Eyre went to the bank to open a personal checking account. By then the teenager had learned how to budget and handle cash. The parents in the interim worked to save for something important, such as a family trip. The Eyres claimed their boys and girls needed that exposure.

The Allans of Richmond, Virginia, have taken a different tack with their three children, Anne Marie, 13, Catherine, 12, and Christopher, 3. Mike, the father, a former treasurer of a Fortune 500 Company, and Nancy, the mother, have instructed each girl to put her earnings and allowance equally in three jars designated charity, savings, and spending. Catherine marked the top of her jars with symbols—a pig for savings, hands for charity, and dollar signs for spending.

The girls tithe to the Mormon church. They each support a youngster in Thailand through the Christian Children's Fund. Anne Marie volunteered how she spent the remaining portion of the third allocated to charity. She said, "I send money to the Red Cross because of my interest in being a candystriper." Catherine contracted meningitis years ago.

While hospitalized she observed a bald, four year boy suffering from cancer. She said, "That led me to send money to St. Jude, a Children's Research Hospital in Memphis." She observed the fruits of her generosity in a visit to the facility with her father.

When the girls became disappointed with the lack of growth in their savings account they invested in Intel. Shortly thereafter the stock dipped, so they diversified into Microsoft and a health care company.

The Third Sense: Fulfillment of the Need to Be Loved

The third sense is one of belonging. Children, parents, and grandparents seek to be cherished. Built into the human psyche is the desire to be loved. Dobson asserts that children should feel that parents "really do care about me," as self-esteem is the most fragile attribute of human nature.

Urie Bronfenbrenner, a longtime professor of psychology and of child development and family studies at Cornell University, paraphrased these sentiments in speaking of the child's need for the "enduring, irrational involvement of one or more adults." When asked to define irrational involvement, he replied, "Somebody has got to be crazy about that kid."

The development of the three senses leads to a mentally and spiritually healthy adult ready to repeat the same process for the next generation. Raising his or her own family should be the most significant experience of that woman's or man's life. The challenge will cause the wife, the mother, and her husband, the father, to increase and build their love for each other. The sinews of the larger society will be strengthened. As President John Adams observed, "The foundation of national morality must be laid in private families." The lessons children learn about saving—the experience of deferred gratification through wanting and waiting—will evidence themselves in the investments adults make in the future. Stable democratic order is founded in the family.

Admiral Richard Byrd spent four months at the South Pole by himself. Death stalked him. He deliberated on the meaning of existence. What really counts. He writes in *Alone,*

> At the end only two things really matter to a man, regardless of who he is: and they are the affection and understanding of his family. Anything and everything else he creates are insubstantial; they are ships given over to the mercy of winds and tides of prejudice. But the family is the everlasting anchorage, a quiet harbor where a man's ships can be left to swing to the moorings of pride and loyalty.

On Neighborhoods

What Makes a Neighborhood?

Six married couples in Richmond, Virginia were winding up an evening's discussion on values in contemporary society when one commented, "I like living here on Willway Avenue. Why were we upset when a newly divorced husband moved down the street and rejected our friendly overtures in getting acquainted? What makes a neighborhood?"

This same question was asked in the Free Access column in a brief revival of *Harper's Weekly*. The writer solicited suggestions for a curriculum for deliberations on the characteristics of a vibrant neighborhood. Nine responses from Woodbury, Connecticut, to Missoula, Montana, recommending seven books arrived, including a letter from the editor of *Planning*, Robert Cassidy, then in the midst of putting together a book on the subject.

Surprisingly, none of the entries concentrated on physical assets, such as the distance to schools and shopping or the availability of public transportation,—measures that a real estate appraiser uses to describe and analyze in assessing their impact on value. The emphasis throughout lay on the relationship between people living near each other.

When the Richmond couples reconvened, after perusing the books suggested, they judged *The Death and Life of*

American Cities by Jane Jacobs and *We, the Lonely People* by Ralph Keyes as most apt to promote insight into the special fabric of the block on which they resided.

Jane Jacobs championed teeming metropolises with dense concentrations of population. She preferred diversity and opted for a neighborhood where people work, shop, and reside on the same block. She observed several characteristics in a vital neighborhood. People cluster about in large numbers in public areas and, in doing so, ensure personal safety. They respect privacy while also enjoying frequent contact outside their residences—especially among children at play as adults watch unobtrusively. Mrs. Jacobs noted, too, the intense attachment among people who have forged ties; stability prevails through self-government and the gradual assimilation of neighbors.

In contrast to Mrs. Jacobs' preference for diversity and mixed uses, the group participants felt the tract, *Studying Your Community* by Roland G. Warren, more appropriate in delineating their block as homogeneous, composed of the "same type of people" all residing in single-family dwellings.

Keyes wrote of the paradox of modern America—people engaged in a romance with the automobile, which satisfies a passion for mobility and convenience. But while Americans like privacy, they search for a sense of community, too. Keyes did not explore neighborhoods with physical boundaries, but viewed them as groups of people, such as hobbyists, with similar interests.

For cohesion he prescribed a personal commitment that dictates exclusivity, manageable size, the acceptance of oppression through standards, and a willingness to stay through friction and temporary abrasions. Keyes lost a sense of intimacy when a group exceeds twelve, and he was satisfied with a community of 500 people where all the inhabitants recognize one another.

The evening discussions led to a consensus on criteria (see pages 111-113) as pertinent to their neighborhood and others they easily recognized in Richmond.

Now for an elaboration on those criteria. The author, a real estate appraiser, observed that the conventional approach to judging the vitality of a neighborhood lay in an assessment of its physical assets and location. In obtaining a sense of a neighborhood, a form published by the American Institute of Real Estate Appraisers calls for a description of a neighborhood's age, the percentage built-up, the type of improvements and transportation facilities.

The Jacobs premise centered on the interaction between individuals. The idea that the "sight of people attracts still other people," a phenomenon Mrs. Jacobs believed city planners found incomprehensible, struck a responsive chord with the Willway participants. The couple agreed with the sentiment implied in the question by Coriolanus, "What is the city but the people?"

Keyes and others like Vance Packard and Alvin Toffler have depicted the increasing mobility in America aptly caught in the title, *A Nation of Strangers*. The mobility, desire for privacy, freedom from ties, commitment to change for change's sake, pursuit of anonymity and passion for convenience all epitomized, Keyes writes, by the automobile and the turnover of one in every five homes in the nation annually, run counter to the idea of togetherness and a sense of community rooted in stability.

Keyes noted, too, that the mobile society allows families to uproot and leave rather than stay and resolve problems whenever disputes occur and friction arises. The Willway residents opted for stability. They observed that in a five-year period residences on the street had changed hands at the rate of one per twenty per year. During the same span, six homeowners had added on rather than move. At least two families had resided on the block since the initial homes had gone up approximately 45 years ago. The late H. Magruder Taylor III, an occasional quipster, had lived on the block as a youth from 1932 to 1956. Now wearing a hearing aid, he had returned in 1968 with a wife and two daughters "to help," he claimed, "reverse any downhill trend."

In a halcyon world we may all love our neighbor. But, Keyes writes, trust is not indiscriminate. In defining a community he asks, "Would anyone notice if I didn't show up?" The question ultimately comes to "how many can you relate to?" Willway Avenue contains 40 homes. We agreed with the brochure publicizing the virtues of a suburban planned community where "you can enjoy the company of good friends and never leave the neighborhood." The developers there declare the neighborhoods of 25 to 75 families to be designed on a smaller scale than most.

People living in roomy houses on spacious lots may prefer privacy to easy association with nearby residents. A father in a nearby manor on an acre lot lamented the absence of children for his tots to romp with. The relative density arising from the 65 foot lots typical of Willway Avenue enabled the 43 children on the block to convene easily while the parents mused on the state of the world on the Parsons' front steps.

The maintenance of standards and values and the existence of shared interests provide the glue cementing groups. Binding ties and hostile threats from outside cause people to band together. Keyes wrote these primal forces effecting human links engender an "acceptance of oppression." The self becomes subordinate to the tyranny of the group.

James D. Davis of nearby Kingcrest Parkway called a

Willway buff and inquired, "How do you get a neighborhood going? We'd like to do what you are doing." He was told that a get-together in which everybody in the vicinity is invited is an ideal device. Thus, the genesis of the first "Kingcrest-Springfest." Rituals are important. John H. Fay, a group participant and Willway's gift to frontier justice when he re-erected a block party barricade that local police had taken down prematurely, said, "A block party offers the opportunity to bring together everyone from one to 90, including the lame, halt, and blind."

Jane Jacobs lauded public areas where people can congregate in an impromptu fashion. She praised small parks, front porches, and streets as sites where the people in the community meet naturally. At the same time, Mrs. Jacobs asserted, "What goes on inside the home is private." Another resident added, "I expect people to ring our doorbell before they enter. They are welcome to come in only after being invited." We concurred with the proposition, the unwritten consensus, that the balance between privacy within the residence and frequent contact without, especially among children, should be respected.

The participants felt the homogeneity of a relatively strict set of standards was at odds with Mrs. Jacobs' preference for diversity. She favored a lack of order. Though there are liberals and conservatives at the ballot box on Willway and Lorraine Abernathy could cite, "We even have a Yankee," those who took part in the discussions were not distraught that they shared similar skin pigmentation, income ranges, and values.

Three years after the completion of the discussions on Willway Avenue, Holt, Rinehart, and Winston published Cassidy's *Livable Cities*. Cassidy had seen the notice in

Harper's Weekly that prompted responses from around the country.

"What exactly is a neighborhood?" Cassidy asked rhetorically in his book. He referred to assorted replies. The National Association of Real Estate Boards had called the entity "hard to define but easily understood." Columnist Murray Kempton said it "is where, when you go out of it, you get beat up." For Cassidy, the neighborhood was a reference point giving him identity. He wrote, "Because I live in a politically conservative, heavily European, largely Catholic neighborhood of Chicago, people have a certain image of me quite different from what it would be if I lived in ultra-hip Old Town or 'academic' Hyde Park."

Cassidy contrasted the physical aspect of a home with the personal sense of place. He cited a woman who came to restore old houses but wound up restoring the neighborhood. He started a paragraph, "People with options don't just buy a house: They buy a neighborhood." Predicate public policy on that perspective. The focus must remain on people, not structures, for houses and neighborhoods only reflect the well-being of the households themselves. A sympathetic soul added, "There is increasing awareness that the future of mature urban neighborhoods is determined far more by interactions among past, present, and future owners than by age or condition of the housing stock itself."

The former *Planning* editor counseled a public policy he dubs humane Darwinism. He advocates survival of the fittest neighborhoods measured not in physical terms but by involvement and organization within the community. Citizens should begin with a plan of their own contrivance. He suggested citizens drop a "we" versus "them" mentality and cooperate with city officials. His stance goes back to Alexis

De Tocqueville, the 19th century commentator from France, who observed,

> The political existence of the majority of nations of Europe commenced in the superior ranks of society, and was gradually and imperfectly communicated to the different members of the social body. In America, on the contrary, it may be said that the township was organized before the county, the county before the State, the State before the Union.

Cassidy also recommended *Building Neighborhood Confidence* by Rolf Goetze for any reading list. Goetze claimed perception outweighs reality. He wrote, "Often the way people view a city or neighborhood is more important than what facts reveal to be the truth." Thus confidence is crucial.

How is confidence measured? By supply and demand. Stable neighborhoods are in balance. Enough willing buyers match sellers who want to sell. In a strong neighborhood demand outstrips the available dwelling units. When this ratio turns, "confidence waxes and the probability of speculation enters; and where it declines, confidence wanes and the likelihood of disinvestment becomes more real."

While confidence is the decisive factor shaping housing dynamics, accessible credit must be present, too. Sellers can't sell, nor buyers buy, without financing. When the buyer/seller ratio drops below an equilibrium point,

> ... the banks' reluctance to grant mortgages and home improvement loans becomes known to real estate brokers and owners. Fewer prospective buyer households consider looking at houses in that market, while more current owners become inclined to sell while they can still "get out their equity."

The establishment of characteristics reminds one of the murky wonderlands in which those trying to fathom "quality education" and "quality of life" have traveled. After one quality of life survey, Overton Jones, an associate editor of *The Richmond Times-Dispatch*, wrote an editorial page column that promoted a respect for the virtue of diffidence. Jones observed that Mobile, Alabama, ranked last in a survey of more than 60 cities on the basis of certain characteristics designed and scrutinized by a mid-western research group.

When the finance commissioner of Mobile was asked for his reaction to the findings, he replied,

> Mobile is the best city in the world in which to live and everybody in Mobile knows that. If somebody in Kansas City can't come up with some statistics to find out why Mobile is the best in the world, that's their problem, not ours.

(The Mobile response is also reminiscent of the black block-association activist from the Bronx who proclaimed, "We the people at the grass roots declare that we care about New York, that we are together, that we are going to stay together and fight together for the survival of the city.")

Neighborhood enthusiasts rhapsodize on not black, or white, or flower, but block power. Spirit matters—hardly measurable or quantifiable. But it matters most.

Some Guidelines

People/Not Facilities. The association between people is more important than such amenities as bus transportation, shopping facilities, and churches.

Stability. People consider a move to the area as long-term rather than interim. They intend to work out problems between themselves rather than withdraw or move.

STRUCTURE. Informal organization (without presiding officers or regularly scheduled meetings), excepting when outside threats occur, causing the creation of an ad hoc group to react for the neighborhood's protection.

NUMBER/SIZE. The area contains clearly identifiable boundaries. Most of the residents would know the names of all of the families within the boundaries. The number of dwelling units would probably not exceed 100.

DENSITY. The lots must necessarily be small enough to promote easy social interchange.

STANDARDS. A belief in upholding certain values. A strong family orientation, attention to property maintenance, an emphasis on civil manners, and a desire to be friendly are cited as possible standards that the total neighborhood would try to encourage.

SHARED INTERESTS. Children, neighborhood schools, religious or ethnic ties are examples. Racial integration feasible when that condition reflects the will of the residents.

RITUALS. Pomp, games and ceremonies in which all within the boundaries are invited.

PUBLIC AREAS. Places where children can play outside residences without direct adult supervision. These sites should be recognized as safe (free from heavy vehicle traffic), where children and adults enjoy personal security. In most instances, the common areas will be visible to adults inside the homes in the neighborhood.

RESPECT FOR PRIVACY. The residents appreciate the others' rights to carry on household activities without abrupt intrusion.

Heterogeneity. Generally more attractive in theory than in practice. Some variation in house design. A mixture of age groups anticipated in stable areas where residents stay for long periods, since parents tend to raise a family and spend their twilight years in the same house.

Spirit. A place or institution in which residents take pride. A feeling that something special prevails about the group as seen by its members.

Why Good Neighborhoods Are Important

Gaylen Cook wrote from Iowa City, Iowa:

> To carve out the niche we all desire to create. We must search out our own *milieu*. Asking why good neighborhoods are important seems to me to be getting the cart before the horse. Rather, the neighborhood is important (to you, to me) because it is good. We all choose where we wish to be, and where we are is fulfilling a need for us. Be glad for what you have.

As school children, we learned of the dedication of our forefathers to life, liberty, and the pursuit of happiness. Many neighborhood buffs link their own enthusiasm for neighborhoods with a sense of well-being and personal joy. Each human aspires to live in a good place. A measure of happiness relates to a group of families we find supportive.

Walter Koostra wrote from Missoula, Montana:

> One sincerely hopes that the neighborhood can be a countervailing force to the social malaise typified by divorce, family transience and breakup, and alcohol and other drug abuse; the neighborhood may diminish the isolation produced by the automobile and television and offer psychological security, which is ever more precious in a changing

> world. Beyond a certain level of the physical necessities of food, shelter, clothing, and perhaps, medical care, we become free to address the real necessities of music, story-telling, dance, drama, play, and worship. The neighborhood may afford an opportunity for development of these—as opposed to the canned-laughter, passive-onlooker variety of recreation. And, in so doing, the neighborhood provides a sense, so wanting today, of actively participating, of counting for something, of belonging, of roots.

The psychological security to which Koostra referred led others to talk of the quest of community. Koostra wondered if his pessimism derives from living in the West, where an "I'm all right, Jack" frontier mentality is more visible—if not more prevalent—than in the East.

More recently, the matter was discussed with individuals who have demonstrated an interest in Richmond neighborhoods. Lee Rice of the Richmond-First Club called the burgeoning revitalization of neighborhoods a welcome contrast to the selfish, laissez-faire individualism and rationalism that are distinctive characteristics of American culture. Another voice waxes enthusiastic about the camaraderie of children working with older people.

According to Frank Gilbert, the prime mover in forming the civic organization in Richmond's Carillon area, people living close to one another have become friends because of mutual involvement in the association's activities, such as the annual art show.

Practical benefits arise from neighborhoods, too. Psychological security and physical security are indissoluble. For some the necessities of story-telling and drama are esoteric; but the need for personal safety and possession of personal property is real. Neighborhood associations are engaged in crime prevention. And they can point to successes. Former City Councilman and Mayor Walter Kenney believes that the

East View Civic Association was instrumental in reducing car thefts and vandalism. The reduction in crime promoted the community's pride, and that pride in turn brought about an increase in property values.

A neighborhood organization provides a mechanism for solving social problems including crime, housing, recreation, and the delivery of municipal services. Doctor James H. Boykin, who holds the Alfred L. Blake Chair of Real Estate at Virginia Commonwealth University, alluded to his own experience in a neighborhood where a civic association garnered 600 signatures on a petition to express concern to the city fathers. He says, "We gain social security from such an association, which acts as a communications device in protecting our interests."

In talking with John Ritchie, the veteran executive director of the Virginia Housing Development Authority, we get an impression of two adjoining sectors of Richmond which offer a study in contrasts between the "I don't care; it's not my problem" attitude and the "We can do it together" stance. Said Ritchie:

> I live on the border between the two neighborhoods. In one, we get to know each other. The children play together. We share problems, such as how do you get your rugs cleaned and what do we do about the dog knocking over the garbage cans. That area is also functioning as a political unit representing common concerns—lighting, garbage collection, traffic plans and patterns, and schools. In contrast, the other area is marginal. Interaction is lacking and relationships between families are absent. The people are suspicious and don't help each other with problems. They have no social outlets, nor do they harness the more anti-social members with dogs tipping over the garbage cans.

A film produced by the National Association of Realtors described the home as "the heart of a nation." The family, the smallest and most important social unit in the country and the world, lives in the home. Anna Soulios, who presided over the local Realtors' Neighborhood Revitalization program, says pride in the home reflects pride in the neighborhood. She points out that the environment immediately outside the residence is of great consequence in raising children.

Pride is pervasive and, according to Kenney, affects the children in their studies by motivating them to work harder. Some parents treasure their heritage and envision themselves as duty-bound to preserve and pass on to their children a part of the past. Gilbert says, "If you grew up in a neighborhood like the one in which I was raised, you see its value and want to preserve something of its nature for your children."

Strong Organizations

First, the individual, then the family, then the neighborhood, and now the city or county. Why is a good neighborhood important to a larger jurisdiction? Kenney claims the future of Richmond lies in strong neighborhood organizations. The lead paragraph in a newspaper article syndicated by George Gallup began,

> Many observers of the urban scene maintain that the survival of America's cities depends to a major extent on the rejuvenation of the neighborhoods. If the decline of the neighborhoods can be arrested, or if the neighborhood quality can be improved, the cities will inevitably benefit.

The argument runs that the whole is equal to—if not greater than—the sum of its parts. The city is composed of a series of building blocks. The stronger the foundations and bone structure in those blocks, the stronger and healthier the city.

Or you can view a city in terms of economics, the retention of a tax base. That is the focus of two persons interviewed on the matter. Jerry Gereaux of Richmond's Planning Department said,

> We've got to have the money to make the whole thing function. Looking at the matter from a person's perspective, few see that upkeep of the home will lead to the funding of the services residents seek. From the city's perspective, we are here because of a demand for a governmental structure to help fill all the needs within a community in which we live. It's difficult to imagine the alternative to a good solid residential base. Total disinvestment would be a disaster. For a city to be a good place to work it has to be a good place to live in.

Community Fabric

Edwin B. Brooks, Jr., former president of Security Federal Savings & Loan Association, talked of the fabric of the community. He related the state of the neighborhood to the state of the metropolitan area. Savings and loan association manifestos invariably hold that the security of the nation lies in the homes of its people, and people become better citizens (they are more likely to vote) when they own their residences. Brooks said,

> I have testified before Senator William Proxmire in emphasizing that we need volunteer effort in promoting neighborhoods. If we let neighborhoods in the inner city deteriorate, the whole area—as far as Hanover County—will be affected. It makes more sense to work with existing neighborhoods and remodel older houses than to undertake new construction. With the problems involving a diminishing supply of cheap energy, we should try to improve what we already have.

Former President Lyndon Johnson proposed a vast legislative program to bring about the "Great Society." The thesis here lies in the belief that the creation of the great society starts with the individual and expands ever outward to family, then neighborhood, then city, state, and nation. Not vice versa.

Bibliography

Ahlstrom, Sydney. *A Religious History of the American People.* New Haven: Yale University Press, 1972.

Arendt, Hannah. *On Revolution.* New York: Viking Press, 1963.

Bennett, William J. *Book of Virtues.* New York: Simon & Schuster; 1993.

Berle, Adolph. *Navigating the Rapids.* New York: Harcourt Brace Jovanovich, 1973.

Brant, Irving. *Bill of Rights: Its Origin and Meaning.* Indianapolis: Bobbs-Merrill, 1965.

Campbell, Joseph. *Hero With a Thousand Faces.* Princeton, N.J.: Princeton University Press, 1972.

Cassidy, Robert. *Livable Cities: a Grass-roots Guide to Rebuilding Urban America.* New York, Holt, Rinehart, and Winston, 1980.

Chambers, Whittaker. *Witness.* New York: Random House, 1952.

Cherrington, David J. *The Work Ethic; Working Values and Values that Work.* New York: Amacon, 1980.

Dobson, James C. *Dare to Discipline.* Wheaton, Illinois: Tyndale House Publishers, 1995.

Durant, Will. *Story of Philosophy.* New York: Simon and Schuster, 1926.

Durant, Will and Ariel. *Story of Civilization.* New York: Simon and Schuster, Volumes VII, VIII, IX, and XI, 1957, 1961, 1963, and 1975.

Eyre, Linda and Richard. *3 Steps to a Strong Family.* New York: Simon and Schuster, 1994.

Franklin, Benjamin. *A Benjamin Franklin Reader*. New York: Thomas Y. Crowell, 1945.

Fromm, Eric. *To Have or To Be?* New York: Harper & Row, 1976.

Fuchs, Victor R. *How We Live.* Cambridge, Mass.: Harvard University Press, 1983.

Gardner, John W. *No Easy Victories*. New York: Harper & Row, 1968.

Gardner, Ralph D. *Horatio Alger, or, the American Hero Era.* Mendota, Illinois, Wayside Press, 1964.

Handlin, Oscar. *Uprooted.* Boston: Little, Brown, 1973.

Hayek, Friedrich A. von. *Road to Serfdom*. Chicago: University of Chicago Press, 1944.

Jacobs, Jane. *The Death and Life of Great American Cities*. New York: Random House, 1961.

James, William. *The Will to Believe and Other Essays*. New York: Dover Publications, 1956.

Keyes, Ralph. *We, the Lonely People; Searching for Community*. New York: Harper & Row, 1973.

Locke, John. *Two Treatises of Civil Government*. New York: Dutton, 1924.

Lorenz, Konrad. *On Aggression.* New York: Harcourt, Brace, and World, 1966.

Maslow, Abraham. *Motivation and Personality.* New York: Harper & Row, 1954. Originally published in Psychological Review, 1943.

Mill, John Stuart. *On Liberty*. New York: Appleton-Century-Crofts, 1947.

Morgan, Edmund S. *The Challenge of the American Revolution.* New York: W.W. Norton, 1976.

Pascal, Blaise. *Pensees.* New York: Pantheon Books, 1965.

Pascarella, Perry. *The New Achievers: Creating a Modern Work Ethic.* New York: Free Press, 1984.

Paton, Alan. *Instrument of Thy Peace.* New York: Seabury Press, 1968.

Popenoe, David. *Life Without Father.* New York: Martin Kessler Books, 1996.

Robinson, Ray. *Iron Horse; Lou Gehrig in His Time.* New York: W.W. Norton, 1990.

Rosenfeld, Harvey. *Iron Man; the Cal Ripken, Jr. Story.* New York: St. Martin's Press, 1995.

Senge, Peter. *The Fifth Discipline.* New York: Doubleday, 1990.

Shipler, David. *Arab and Jew.* New York: New York Times Books. 1986.

Smith, Adam. *Wealth of Nations.* New York: P. F. Collier & Son, 1905.

Stillman, Edmund; William Pfaff. *Politics of Hysteria.* New York: Harper & Row, 1964.

Terkel, Studs. *Working.* New York: Pantheon Books, 1974.

Thoreau, Henry. *Walden, and Civil Disobedience.* Boston: Houghton Mifflin, 1960.

Tillich, Paul. *Courage to Be.* New Haven: Yale University Press, 1952.

———. *Dynamics of Faith.* New York: Harper, 1956.

Toqueville, Alexis de. *Democracy in America.* New York: A. A. Knopf, 1945.

Warren, Roland E. *Studying Your Community.* New York: Russell Sage Foundation, 1955.

Weber, Max. *Protestant Ethic and the Spirit of Capitalism.* New York: Scribner, 1976.

Whitehead, Barbara Dafoe. *The Divorce Culture.* New York: Alfred Knopf, 1996.

Wilson, James Q. *The Moral Sense.* New York: Free Press, 1993.

Wilson, James and Herrnstein, Richard J. *Crime and Human Nature.* New York: Simon and Schuster, 1986.

Pamphlets, tracts, and special interest publications in sequence by chapter

Pacem in Terris. Papal Encyclical, 1963.

Colloquium in Response. 1965. Center for Democratic Institutions.

A band of 100-150 members of Mensa known as Peace-Sig contributed to *Peace Notes* edited by Jean Flores of Brooklyn, New York and Charles Obler of Farmville, Virginia. The chapter on peace published in *Peace Notes* editions in 1993 and 1994.

Mihailov, Mihailo. *The Mystical Experience of Loss of Freedom*; from *Underground Notes,* Routledge & Kegan.

Jay C. Wood edited a quarterly publication for liberty enthusiasts in Mensa from 1987 to 1989. Ardell L. Taylor of Patagonia, Arizona, and Jorj Strumulo of Warwick, Rhode Island, edited and improved this essay prior to its publication in July, 1991.

Finn, Chester E.,Jr. *Ten Tentative Truths*; Center of the American Experiment.

Nicholi, Armand M., Jr. M.D. *What Do We Know about Successful Families?*

Massachusetts Mutual Life Insurance Company. *Teaching Family Values-A Two Way Street.*

Newspaper Articles

The majority of the essay on what makes a good neighborhood was published in the Sunday Commentary section of the *Richmond Times-Dispatch* on July 17, 1977. The *Richmond News-Leader* carried the section on why good neighborhoods are important on its editorial page on November 24, 1978.

Interviews

As a Christian attempting to live a Christ-centered life I am responsible for statements of that faith. Saul Viener and Rabbi Lawrence Schlesinger of the Beth Ahabah congregation in Richmond, Virginia, provided me with books, papers, and discussions of the faith of the Jews. Jamel Abed of Richmond did likewise for the faith of Moslems.

Index

K

L

M

N

O

P

R

❧ ❧ ❧

Photo by Dementi-Foster Studios

JIM DOHERTY appreciates the liberal education that led to this work. His education included Classical High School in Springfield, Massachusetts, Deerfield Academy, Bowdoin College, and, professionally, Columbia Business School.

He sold Fuller Brushes in Harlem between his years at Columbia. He moved with a growing family to Richmond, Virginia, thirty-five years ago and now appraises commercial property.

A liberal education provokes an abiding curiosity and abundant interest manifested in the life of the author, who devoted four years to the Great Books program—sponsored by the public libraries—carried the Olympic torch in 1996, received the Good Government Award conferred by the Richmond First Club, and served as president of the Virginia Writers Club for three terms.

Doherty and his wife now anticipate the birth of their sixth grandchild. The author intends, through this book—ten years in the making—to excite you about the prospect of living in this glorious land, and he seeks to encourage you to strengthen the foundations for his and your descendants.

To order additional books, please use coupon below.

Mail or fax to:

Brunswick Publishing Corporation
1386 LAWRENCEVILLE PLANK ROAD
LAWRENCEVILLE, VIRGINIA 23868
Tel: 804-848-3865 • Fax: 804-848-0607
www.brunswickbooks.com

Order Form

❑ ***In The Beginnings: Foundations for the Millenium Ahead***
by James L. Doherty
$12.95 ea., paperback .... $ ____________

Total, books .... $ ____________
VA residents add 4.5% sales tax .... $ ____________
Shipping – within U.S. and Canada
$4.50 first copy .... $ ____________
$.50 ea. additional copy .... $ ____________

Total .... $ ____________

❑ Check enclosed.

❑ Charge to my credit card:
❑ VISA ❑ MasterCard ❑ American Express

Card #________________________________ Exp. Date __________

Signature: ____

Name ____

Address ____

City______________________________ State______ Zip ____________

Phone # ____